Through Cloud and Sunshine

William A. Lauterbach

Concordia Publishing House
St. Louis

COVER PHOTO: "Sunset on Wisconsin River" by Jim Freiberg, "Magnolia in Bloom" by Jack Zehrt—12; "Melting Snow & Icicles" by Josef Muench—16; "Wooded Area" by Frank Silkey—25; "White River in Missouri Ozarks" by Jack Zehrt—32; "Christmas Cactus" by Joan E. Rahn—65; "Winter Morn at Bridgeport, Calif" by Josef Muench—72; "Crocus—First Sign of Spring" by Louis Williams—81; "Mission Bells in Tularosa, N. Mexico" by Fred Ragsdale—92.

The Bible quotations in this publication from the Revised Standard Version [RSV] of the Bible, copyrighted 1946, 1952, © 1971, 1973 by the Division of Christian Education of the National Council of the Churches of Christ in the U.S.A. and those from Today's English Version [TEV] are used by permission. Undesignated Bible quotations are as a rule from the King James Version [KJV].

Copyright © 1979 by Concordia Publishing House
3558 South Jefferson Avenue, St. Louis, MO 63118

All rights reserved. No portion of this book may be reproduced in any form whatsoever, except for brief quotations in reviews, without the written permission of the publisher.

Printed in the United States of America

Library of Congress Cataloging in Publication Data

Lauterbach, William August, 1903-
    Through cloud and sunshine.

    Meditations.
    1. Meditations. I. Title.
BV4832.2.L346   242'.6'5   78-13545
ISBN 0-570-03056-0

TO MY DAUGHTER
Carol Brandt

O God, our Help in ages past,
   Our Hope for years to come,
Our Shelter from the stormy blast,
   And our eternal Home!

Under the shadow of Thy throne
   Thy saints have dwelt secure;
Sufficient is Thine arm alone,
   And our defense is sure.

Before the hills in order stood
   Or earth received her frame,
From everlasting Thou art God,
   To endless years the same.

A thousand ages in Thy sight
   Are like an evening gone,
Short as the watch that ends the night
   Before the rising sun.

Time, like an ever-rolling stream,
   Bears all its sons away;
They fly forgotten as a dream
   Dies at the opening day.

Our God, our Help in ages past
   Our Hope for years to come,
Be Thou our Guard while troubles last
   And our eternal Home!

—Isaac Watts

Contents

Through Cloud and Sunshine	9
Our Stronghold in the Day of Trouble	10
Trust in the Lord	13
The Incomparable Ways of God	15
One Day at a Time	19
Doing HIS Will	21
We Wish to See Jesus	23
Rooted in Christ	26
Jesus, King Most Wonderful	29
The Wondrous Cross	33
What Shall I Do with Jesus?	35
Open the Door	37
Afar Off	40
One of Them	42
Jesus Loved Him	45
He Touched Him	47
For Me	49
Not Ashamed of Us	51
The Common People	54
What a Wonderful God!	57
Walking with God	59
Glorify God	60
Sing to the Lord	64
Bliss Beyond Compare	68
Imperishable Treasure	71
The Hope of Glory	74
Heart Transplant	76
Live Worthy of the Gospel	78
Unprofitable Gain	79

Fatal Neglect	82
The Cloak of Humility	84
What Is Truth?	86
But Not	88
What Time Is It?	90
Amen	94

Through Cloud and Sunshine

The Lord . . . covers the heavens with clouds, He prepares rain for the earth, He makes grass grow upon the hills.

Ps. 147:6-8

Last evening the day came to a close with a gorgeous sunset, and this morning I was greeted by a beautiful sunrise. Both were the result of just the right amount and distribution of clouds in the sky to reflect the sunlight. With heavier clouds the sun would not have broken through, and without any clouds the colorful display would have been missing.

These brilliant displays in the sky brought to mind the parting words of a wise old shut-in that I visited years ago in a home for the aged. Out of a rich experience and a deep faith there came the congenial wish: "May your life have just enough clouds to make a glorious sunset."

Altogether, the resplendent exhibition of clouds and sunshine, coupled with the remembrance of the well-wishes of long ago, give me a more pleasant perspective to a rather difficult night that I have just gone through.

Cloud and sunshine, that is the Lord's pattern for our lives, even as it is for the weather. Both are necessary and important, and in proper balance they supplement each other and enhance the value of life. Just as all sunshine and cloudless skies produce sparse vegetation or barren deserts, so continual clear and cloudless days in life tend to wither mutual deeds of love and sometimes shrivel and destroy faith. On the other hand, prolonged periods of storm and clouds, without a break in the skies, be it in the weather or in the course of our lives, can cause gloom and discouragement. But when sunshine, clouds, and rain are sent in proper proportion, grass will grow upon the hills, orchards and vineyards will bear abundant fruit, and fields yield bountiful crops to provide food for man and beast, and all creation will rejoice in the wonderful blessings of God.

> There's not a plant nor flower below
> But makes Thy glories known;
> And clouds arise and tempests blow
> By order from Thy throne.

Our heavenly Father measures clouds and sunshine for us in accordance with His fatherly love, and whatever He sends us must work out for our good for time and eternity.

> I need Thy presence every passing hour;
> What but Thy grace can foil the Tempter's power?
> Who like Thyself my guide and stay can be?
> Through cloud and sunshine, oh, abide with me!

Our Stronghold in the Day of Trouble

The Lord is good, a Stronghold in the day of trouble; and He knoweth them that trust in Him.

Nah. 1:7

Trouble is the universal experience of mankind. Everyone has a burden to bear, and often some secret heartache, too. Every day has its cares and anxieties, but there come days when these seem to grow and multiply. Misfortune strikes, conflicts develop, hopes are shattered, injustice seems to prevail, sickness and sorrow come, and these days stand out in our lives as "days of trouble."

The child of God is not immune to trouble. Sin is the one great trouble and the source of all other troubles. Scripture says: "We must through much tribulation enter into the kingdom of God" (Acts 14:22). Not only is a person often unable to cope with his troubles alone, but human friends and companions also can offer little help. They cannot still our fears or stop our tears. But there is no need to be dismayed, for we know that we need not face our troubles alone or depend on inadequate sources of help. God is our Stronghold and unfailing Refuge in the day of trouble.

In the days of the prophet Nahum the cities were built with thick stone walls for protection, and in time of danger the people from the surrounding area would flee there for refuge from the enemy. The prophet reminds the people that their real safety was not to be found in walls of stone, but in the protection of God. Nor does Nahum stand alone in so portraying God. The Psalmist says: "God is our Refuge and Strength, a very present Help in trouble" (Ps. 46:1).

The almighty God will amply meet all needs and requirements of His own. He is a sure and certain help, no matter how great and overwhelming the trouble may appear. The greatest national and international calamities are not beyond His power of deliverance for His children. On the other hand, our personal problems and troubles are not too small and insignificant for Him to be concerned about. Indeed, He invites us to come to Him with our troubles to have Him take care of them. He says: "Call upon Me in the day of trouble; I will deliver thee, and thou shalt glorify Me" (Ps. 50:15).

We do well to accept the invitation that He so graciously extends and avail ourselves of His deliverance from all our troubles. This, of course,

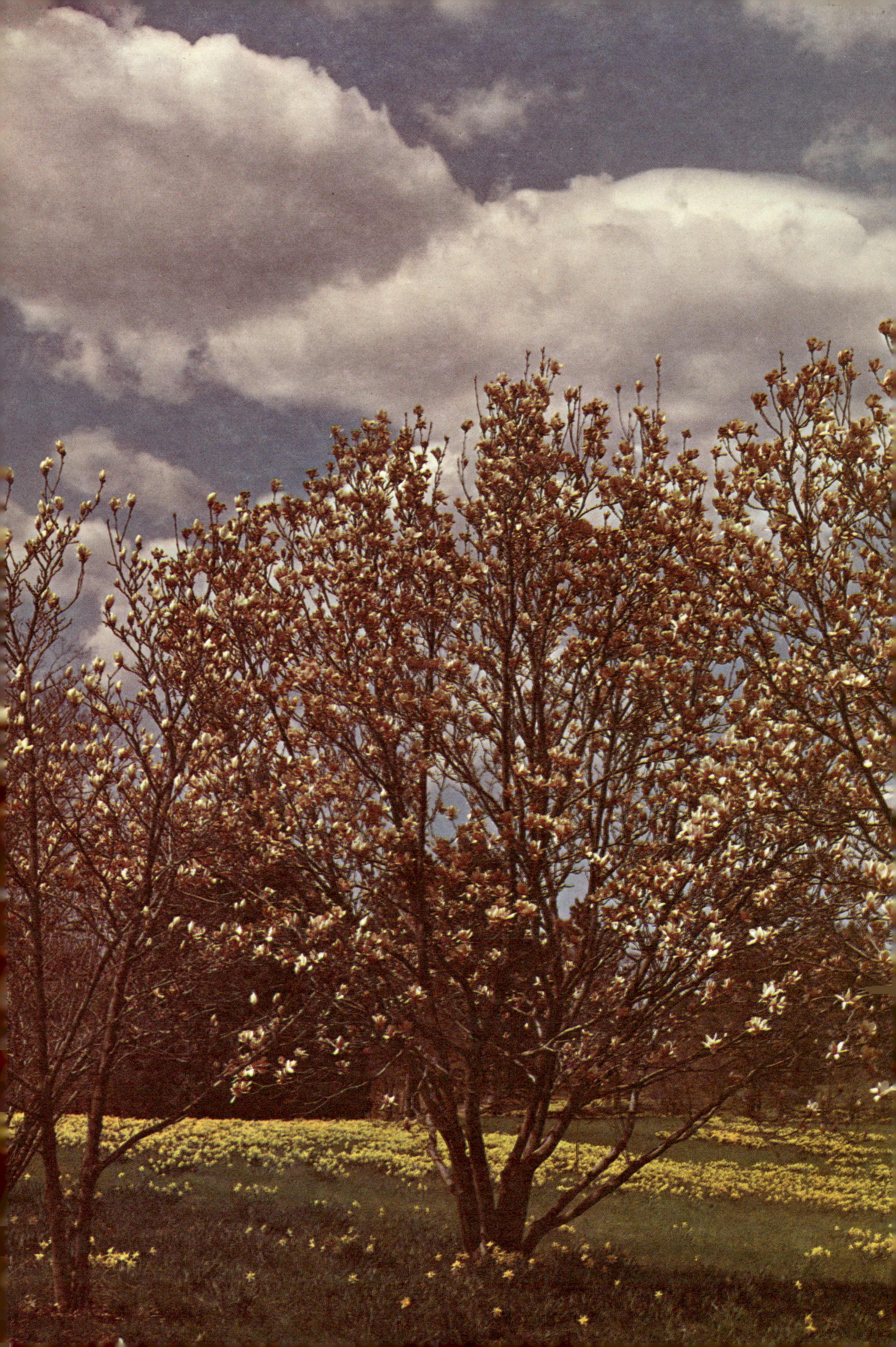

includes our burden of sin. When Satan arouses our conscience and condemns us, God is a sure Stronghold, where we are safe from the attacks of the evil foe. For the sake of Jesus, who suffered and died for us, He will not permit us to perish. He will rescue us, receive us as His own dear children, and provide a safe refuge for us.

> Lead me, and forsake me never,
> Guide my wanderings by Thy Word;
> As Thou hast been, be Thou ever
> My Defense, my Refuge, Lord.
> Never safe except with Thee,
> Thou my faithful Guardian be.

Trust in the Lord

Trust in the Lord with all thine heart; and lean not unto thine own understanding. In all thy ways acknowledge Him, and He shall direct thy paths.

Prov. 3:5-6

> Frail children of dust
> And feeble as frail,
> In Thee do we trust
> Nor find Thee to fail.
> Thy mercies, how tender,
> How firm to the end,
> Our Maker, Defender,
> Redeemer, and Friend!

In this our age of vastly expanding knowledge and growing technology no one is able to acquire more than a fraction of either in a lifetime. More than ever there is need for wisdom to make good use of them, and to properly apply them to the different situations that arise in our day-to-day living, as well as on special circumstances that confront us.

Trusted friends and associates can often advise us, but it is risky to lean too heavily on them, for their knowledge too is limited, and their wisdom fallible. What we really need is a higher degree of knowledge and a more reliable source of wisdom. That can only come from above, from the omniscient God, who has revealed it to us in the Sacred Scriptures. There we are directed to "trust in the Lord" for both knowledge and wisdom that are completely adequate and reliable.

We Americans like to boast that we trust the Lord our God and we have inscribed the motto, "IN GOD WE TRUST", on our coins and currency. Oh, if it were only always true!

Real trust in the Lord is not careless or halfhearted. That is why we read: "Trust in the Lord with all thine heart." Only when trust is done wholeheartedly is it real trust and not just a poor imitation and a sham.

We can confidently trust the Lord, for He is completely trustworthy. He will never fail us or let us down. Human helpers may have good intentions, but they are not always able to deliver. God keeps His promises, and He will direct the paths of those who trust in Him.

By way of contrast we are told: "Lean not unto thine own understanding." Flawed by sin, limited and faulty, our own understanding can easily lead us to choose unwisely. We are especially prone to concentrate too much on bodily and earthly things while neglecting or even forgetting the "things above."

Our paths do not only lead from home to the place of work or recreation, to the school, or the marketplace, and finally to the cemetery. Our paths, like Asaph's, also lead to the sanctuary of God, where we learn His Word for the strengthening of our faith and for preparation for the way to heaven. With him we can confess, "Thou shalt guide me with Thy counsel, and afterward receive me to glory" (Ps. 73:24). How sad that so many make the fatal mistake of leaning on their own understanding to find the way to heaven. They reason that salvation must be merited or earned by character or behavior, rather than trusting the free grace of God, which assures us: "By grace are ye saved through faith; and that not of yourselves: it is the gift of God: not of works, lest any man should boast" (Eph. 2:8-9).

May we confidently and wholeheartedly trust God to direct our paths through and around besetting dangers until we reach the goal of eternal life.

> God of grace and love and blessing,
> Thine alone shall be the praise;
> Give us hearts to trust Thee truly,
> Hands to serve Thee all our days.
> Lord, bestow Thy future blessing
> Till we join the heav'nly host,
> There to praise and serve Thee ever,
> Father, Son, and Holy Ghost.

The Incomparable Ways of God

My thoughts are not your thoughts, neither are your ways My ways, saith the Lord. For as the heavens are higher than the earth, so are My ways higher than your ways, and My thoughts than your thoughts.

Is. 55:8-9

In their context these words refer to the ways in which sinners are justified before God and made citizens of heaven. On this subject God declares, Your ways are not My ways. "As the heavens are higher than the earth, so are My ways higher than your ways."

The human way is to claim God's favor and

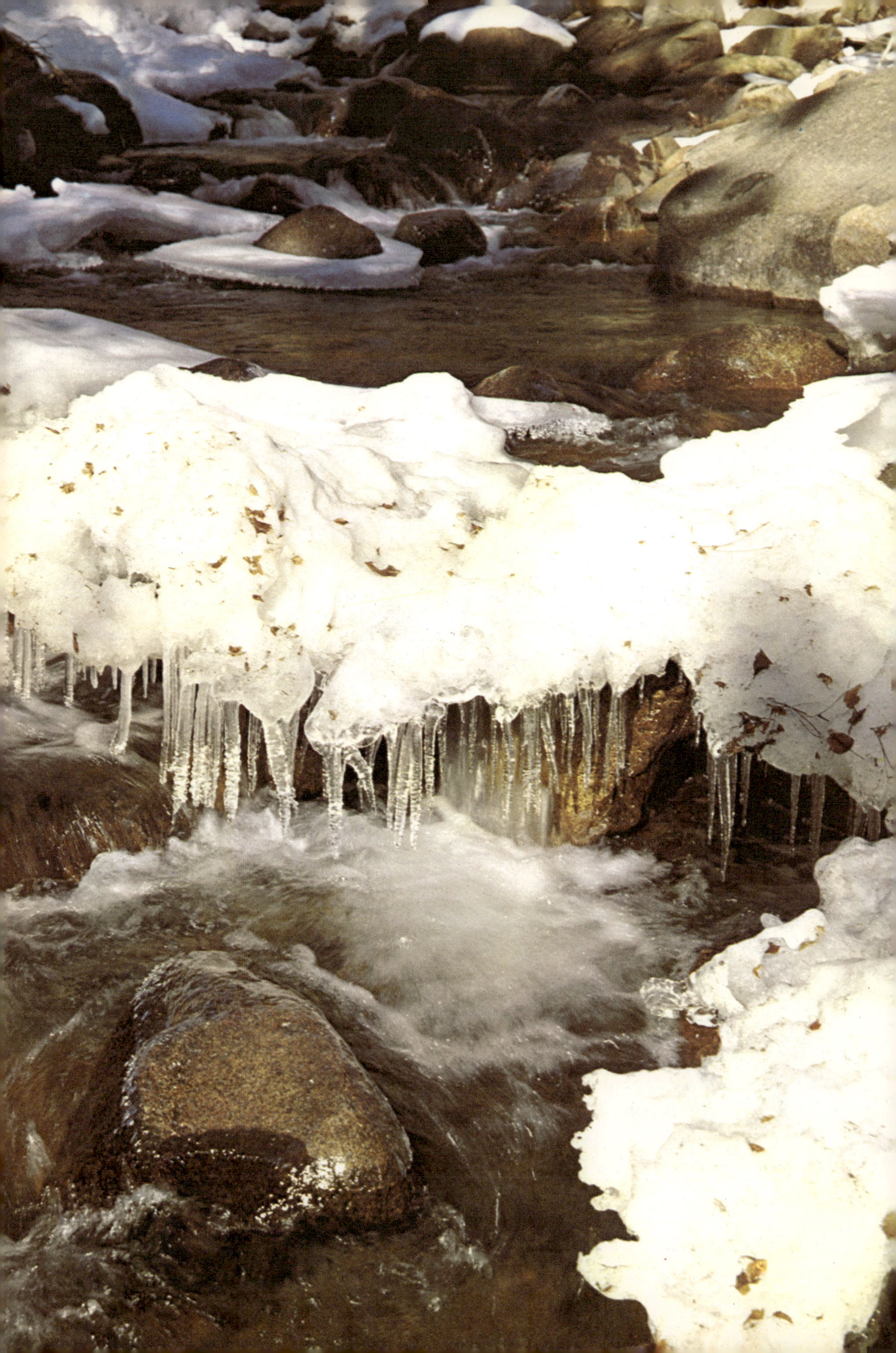

includes our burden of sin. When Satan arouses our conscience and condemns us, God is a sure Stronghold, where we are safe from the attacks of the evil foe. For the sake of Jesus, who suffered and died for us, He will not permit us to perish. He will rescue us, receive us as His own dear children, and provide a safe refuge for us.

> Lead me, and forsake me never,
> Guide my wanderings by Thy Word;
> As Thou hast been, be Thou ever
> My Defense, my Refuge, Lord.
> Never safe except with Thee,
> Thou my faithful Guardian be.

Trust in the Lord

Trust in the Lord with all thine heart; and lean not unto thine own understanding. In all thy ways acknowledge Him, and He shall direct thy paths.

Prov. 3:5-6

> Frail children of dust
> And feeble as frail,
> In Thee do we trust
> Nor find Thee to fail.
> Thy mercies, how tender,
> How firm to the end,
> Our Maker, Defender,
> Redeemer, and Friend!

In this our age of vastly expanding knowledge and growing technology no one is able to acquire more than a fraction of either in a lifetime. More than ever there is need for wisdom to make good use of them, and to properly apply them to the different situations that arise in our day-to-day living, as well as on special circumstances that confront us.

Trusted friends and associates can often advise us, but it is risky to lean too heavily on them, for their knowledge too is limited, and their wisdom fallible. What we really need is a higher degree of knowledge and a more reliable source of wisdom. That can only come from above, from the omniscient God, who has revealed it to us in the Sacred Scriptures. There we are directed to "trust in the Lord" for both knowledge and wisdom that are completely adequate and reliable.

We Americans like to boast that we trust the Lord our God and we have inscribed the motto, "IN GOD WE TRUST", on our coins and currency. Oh, if it were only always true!

Real trust in the Lord is not careless or halfhearted. That is why we read: "Trust in the Lord with all thine heart." Only when trust is done wholeheartedly is it real trust and not just a poor imitation and a sham.

We can confidently trust the Lord, for He is completely trustworthy. He will never fail us or let us down. Human helpers may have good intentions, but they are not always able to deliver. God keeps His promises, and He will direct the paths of those who trust in Him.

By way of contrast we are told: "Lean not unto thine own understanding." Flawed by sin, limited and faulty, our own understanding can easily lead us to choose unwisely. We are especially prone to concentrate too much on bodily and earthly things while neglecting or even forgetting the "things above."

Our paths do not only lead from home to the place of work or recreation, to the school, or the marketplace, and finally to the cemetery. Our paths, like Asaph's, also lead to the sanctuary of God, where we learn His Word for the strengthening of our faith and for salvation in heaven as a reward for one's own good intentions and works of righteousness. However, that way is doomed to failure from the outset, for all human efforts, whether attempts to fulfill all the requirements of God's holy law, or self-imposed sacrifices and tortures, simply cannot pay the penalty for sin. Scripture says, "There is no difference: for all have sinned, and come short of the glory of God" (Rom. 3:22-23), and, "There is not a just man upon earth that doeth good and sinneth not" (Eccl. 7:20). To rely on this way leaves a person hopeless and helpless before the righteous judgment of God.

It takes a better way to reach the heavenly goal, and that is God's way. The higher way of God is the urgent invitation to come and accept the free blessings that He offers so richly and abundantly. All who forget their own imperfect merit and listen to the gracious invitation are promised life and an everlasting covenant with God (Is. 55:1-3). Fulfillment of the promise came when Jesus kept all the demands of the divine Law and gave Himself as a sacrifice for the sins of the world.

These words also teach a general truth applying to various circumstances.

They may apply to the rule that God has laid down for us to follow in His commandments. The "Old Adam" in us rebels against the Law and determines to go his own way. This self-willed way led man into disobedience and sin and continues to lead astray from God. By contrast, the way of God's commandments is a better and more beneficial way, designed by our loving Lord to promote our temporal and eternal welfare.

A more common usage of the term *way* is to apply it to our journey through life from the cradle to the grave. We commonly think of this as the way that has been determined for us by God. Oftentimes this way may not be of our own choosing and sometimes not to our liking. Instead of comfort and ease we may find labor and hardship. Joy and pleasure frequently give way to tribulation and sorrow, and we are apt to cry out, "Why, Lord?"

We know that sin is the basic reason for all of our troubles and griefs. We suffer many heartaches because we neglect to seek God's guidance, or fail to listen to His directions. We do not follow well where He wants to lead us. It would be good to pray as the Psalmist did: "Show me Thy ways, O Lord, teach me Thy paths" (Ps. 25:4), for His ways are indeed higher than our ways, and His thoughts than our thoughts. We can trust Him to choose the right way for us.

We may be so absorbed with the perils and difficulties of the present or so filled with fear of the dark valleys that we must pass through, that it appears certain to us that we are on the wrong road. But our Lord sees the destination at the end of the road and will bring us safely home. And if it means laying a cross upon us to keep us close to him, we can rest assured that He always has our eternal welfare in mind. He is willing to lead us by the hand if we will only trust Him and cling to Him. He will give us an inner peace and sweet comfort that will bring lasting satisfaction.

> Thy ways, O Lord, with wise design
> Are framed upon Thy throne above,
> And ev'ry dark and bending line
> Meets in the center of Thy love.

> Be still, my soul; thy best, thy heav'nly Friend
> Bear patiently the cross of grief or pain;
> Leave to thy God to order and provide;
> In ev'ry change He faithful will remain.
> Be still, my soul; they best, thy heav'nly Friend
> Through thorny ways leads to a joyful end.

One Day at a Time

Take no thought, saying, What shall we eat? or, What shall we drink? or, Wherewithal shall we be clothed? (For after all these things do the Gentiles seek:) for your heavenly Father knoweth that ye have need of all these things. But seek ye first the kingdom of God and His righteousness; and all these things shall be added unto you. Take therefore no thought for the morrow: for the morrow shall take thought for the things of itself. Sufficient unto the day is the evil thereof.

Matt. 6:31-34

Hard as we may try otherwise, we can live only one day at a time, and that day is always today. Yesterday is past and gone and nothing we can do will bring it back or change it. And the future is no more ours than the past. We may plan for tomorrow and prepare ourselves for the days and years to come, but it is impossible to live in them, for when the tomorrows come they will be today. Only today is ours, a gift from our Lord and God, to be used according to His will and purpose.

But we are often not content to live according to that rule. Instead we worry about the past and fret and stew about the future. It is foolish to cling to the troubles of the past or to bring the burdens of tomorrow into today. Our shoulders are not strong enough to carry the burdens of more than one day at a time—and only with strength that comes from above.

Jesus knew and understood the need and concerns of everyday living. He urged people to live one day at a time and not to worry about the future. "Take no thought for the morrow," He said, "Sufficient unto the day is the evil thereof." In the Sermon on the Mount He also taught us to pray: "Give us this day our daily bread" (Matt. 6:11). We are not to be apprehensive about the future. Instead He pleads with us to live one day at a time, trustingly, aware that the throne of grace is accessible to us every day of our lives.

Worry and anxiety about the future not only add to our burden and rob us of our contentment and joy, but also indicate a lack of faith and trust in the heavenly Father, who has promised to take care of us. His resources are boundless and more than ample for all our necessities.

There are more important needs for us than food, clothing, and shelter. Greater by far than these is our need for "the kingdom of God and His righteousness," for these concern the salvation of our immortal soul. Seeking them should be our first and foremost concern each and every day. If we do so, putting first things first, we have the added promise that God will also provide for our lesser needs. The Lord's unfailing love and mercy shall continue. They are new every morning, as sure as the sunrise. His faithfulness and love assure us of provision, care, and deliverance today. That is all we need. When tomorrow comes, that will then again be today, and His care will still be present. So we commend ourselves into His gracious keeping, casting all our care upon Him, for He cares for us. (1 Peter 5:7)

>   The Lord, my God, be praised,
>   My Light, my Life from heaven;
>   My Maker, who to me
>   Hath soul and body given;
>   My Father, who doth shield
>   And keep me day by day,
>   Doth make each moment yield
>   New blessings on my way.

Doing HIS Will

I came down from heaven, not to do Mine own will, but the will of Him that sent Me.

John 6:38

Jesus came into this world on a momentous mission. His assignment from the heavenly Father was to redeem lost and condemned mankind from the consequences of self-willed transgression of God's command. Discharging the task called for total commitment to His Father's will. Time and again He declared this as the purpose of His life. It was a goal that He fulfilled perfectly from the beginning to the close of His earthly life. It involved much more than resignation and patient submission to suffering and abuse. It was first and foremost a *doing* or performance.

Every day, every moment, He was *doing* the Father's will. In the home, at school, in the carpenter shop, while teaching and preaching, while healing or comforting, in the temple, on the mountain, by the Sea of Galilee, at the wedding festivities at Cana, at dinner in the house of Simon, the Pharisee—whereever He was, He was always intent on doing God's will; never doing anything else. At the tender age of 12 Jesus told his worried parents, "How is it that ye sought Me? wist ye not that I must be about My Father's business?" (Luke 2:49) During His public ministry His answered His critics, "I seek not Mine own will, but the will of the Father which hath sent Me" (John 5:30).

While primarily active in *doing* the Father's will, He was likewise ready to submit to it under intense suffering. In Gethsemane He prayed: "O My Father, if it be possible, let this cup pass from Me; nevertheless not as I will, but as Thou wilt" (Matt. 26:39), and on the cross

He patiently endured all the pain and scorn inflicted on Him.

Intent on doing the Father's will Himself, Jesus also wanted the disciples to follow in His footsteps. He taught them to pray: "Thy will be done in earth, as it is in heaven" (Matt. 6:10). He likewise asks all who acknowledge Him as their Lord and Master to *do* the Father's will at all times. That means doing everything that He would have us do in accordance with His Word and in obedience to His command. It requires willing and loving service for God and our fellowmen, rather than wilfully and deliberately going the way of our own selfish, sinful human inclination. Furthermore, it calls for a cheerful submission to His gracious will in the days of adversity, with full trust and confidence in His constant love and concern. And while that loving concern may seem far away in times of special need, sorrow, and affliction, and we may wonder why it must be so, we know that He is always concerned with what is best for us, and that He will not leave us nor forsake us.

If we truly succeed in yielding our will to the will of our heavenly Father when the pressures of adversity put our faith to the test, then we will share the triumph of victory over temptation with our Lord and Savior.

> Oh, that the Lord would guide my ways
> To keep His statutes still!
> Oh, that my God would grant me grace
> To know and do His will!

We Wish to See Jesus

Now among those who went up to worship at the feast were some Greeks. So these came to Philip, who was from Bethsaida in Galilee, and said to him, "Sir, we wish to see Jesus."

John 12:20-21 RSV

The request of a number of Greeks to see Jesus was more than a desire to get a look at a prominent public figure. Unlike the desire of many in that festive multitude of Passover celebrants at Jerusalem who hoped to satisfy their curiosity by getting a glimpse of the famous "rabbi" that so many people were talking about, theirs was a deeper longing, and that is why John reports the incident in his Gospel.

These Greeks were only a very small fragment of the huge crowd of worshipers at the festival, but who they were and what they sought is significant and worthy of our attention.

They were Gentiles who through contact with their neighbors, or otherwise, had accepted the Jewish faith and placed their hope in the Messiah. Though their participation in worship, as "proselytes of the gate," was restricted, they had come to Jerusalem to celebrate the Passover at the Temple. The fame of Jesus' teachings and works awakened their interest and raised the question in their minds whether He was possibly the promised Messiah, as some were saying. To find an answer to their question, the Greeks sought help from Philip, a disciple of Jesus.

It is noteworthy that at the beginning of the earthly career of Jesus, Gentile magi from the East sought Jesus, and now again, at the close, Gentiles came to find Him. It recalls the prophecy of Simeon at the presentation of Jesus in the Temple, that the Christ Child was not only to be the glory of His people, Israel, but also a Light to lighten the Gentiles.

This plea of the Greek Gentiles to see Jesus reflects the universal desire of God's people through the ages. We witness this in the ancient patriarchs reverently standing before their smoking altars, as they longed to see the fulfillment of the promises of the coming Messiah, as well as in the Jewish shepherds and Gentile Wise Men who went to Bethlehem to find Him. During the time of His public ministry countless people went out of their way to see Him. Wherever He went the people came, some merely out of curiosity, but many were moved by a deeper interest in Him. These were looking for His help for their bodily and spiritual needs.

The wish to see Jesus has continued down through the centuries and is also prevalent today. And while we must forego looking into His compassionate eyes and gazing upon His sympathetic face, we *can* see Him with the eyes of faith as He has revealed Himself to us in His holy Word.

It means to see Jesus as the eternal Son of God, made flesh to dwell among us as our brother, and to draw us closer to our kind and loving heavenly Father.

It means to see Jesus as our Savior, promised by the Father, foretold by the prophets, proclaimed by angels, and proven by His works; who rendered perfect obedience, fulfilling all the demands of the Law, and, as the Lamb of God, enduring sacrificial suffering and death for us.

It means to see Jesus as the triumphant victor over sin, death, and the devil, who by His triumphant resurrection gave full and sufficient proof of His Messianic claims.

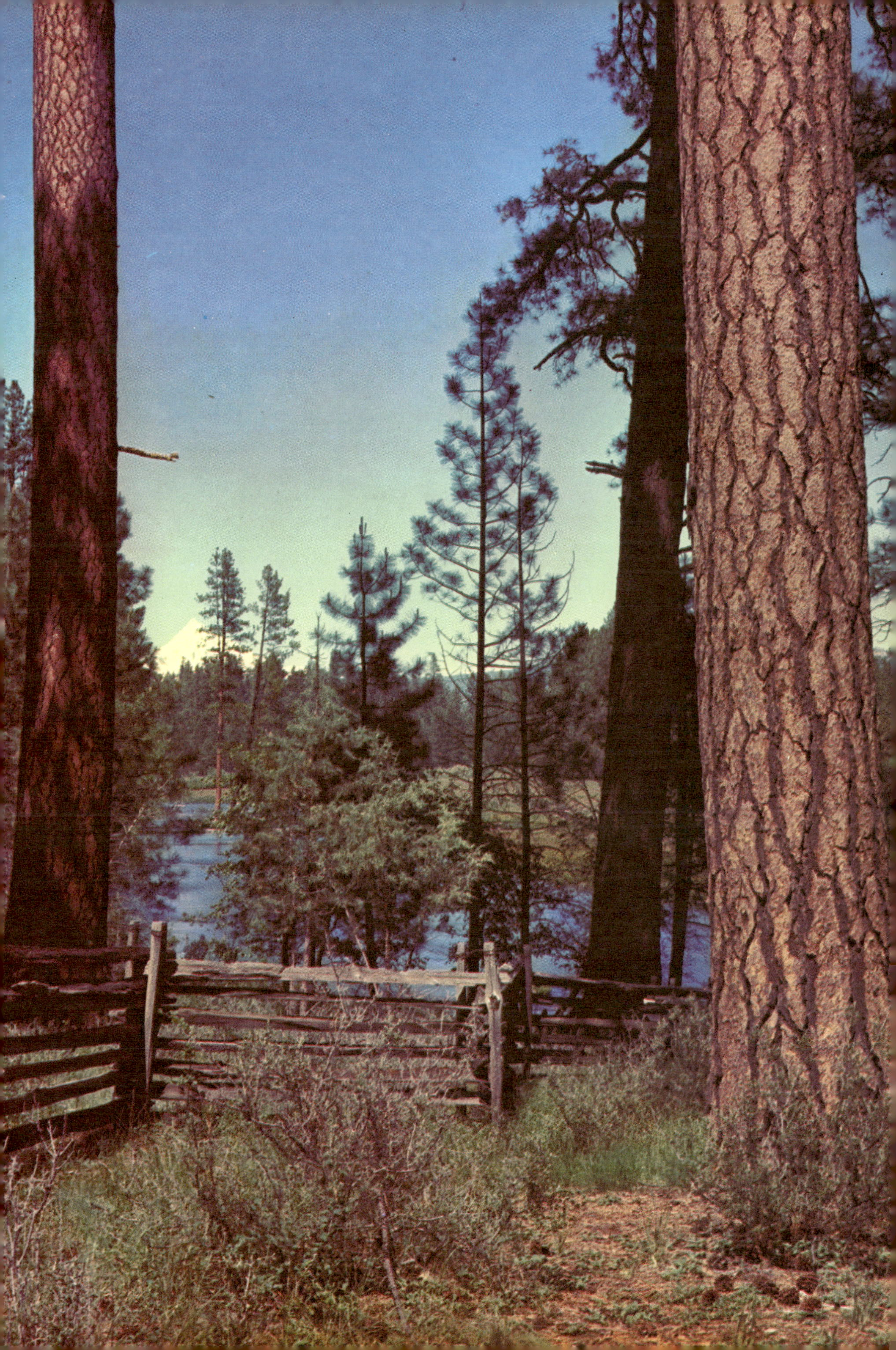

It means to see Jesus as the exalted Lord, sitting at the right hand of the Father, and Lord of the church, who will come again to judge the living and the dead.

To see Jesus thus will satisfy the longing of the heart as nothing else can. It will give a peace that passes all understanding.

> O Love, how cheering is Thy ray!
> All pain before Thy presence flies;
> Care, anguish, sorrow, melt away
> Where'er Thy healing beams arise.
> O Jesus, nothing may I see,
> Nothing desire or seek but Thee!
>
> Oh, draw me, Savior, e'er to Thee;
> So shall I run and never tire.
> With gracious words still comfort me;
> Be Thou my Hope, my sole Desire.
> Free me from every guilt and fear;
> No sin can harm if Thou art near.

Rooted in Christ

Rooted and built up in Him [Christ] and stablished in the faith.

Col. 2:7

How vividly the relationship of the believer to Christ is here illustrated! As a tree is rooted in the soil from which it draws nourishment to grow, thrive, blossom, and bear fruit, so the Christian's faith draws its life-giving and sustaining capability from Christ. In Christ he finds the spiritual nourishment to grow from a small and delicate seedling into a strong and sturdy tree, able to blossom forth and to bear an abundance of God-pleasing fruit.

As being well rooted enables a tree to withstand

severe storms, so being firmly rooted in Christ empowers the believer to withstand the winds of adversity and the fierce storms that threaten to destroy his faith.

When we study the New Testament we soon learn that being "in Christ" is the very heart and center of every phase of our relationship with God. That we are now rooted *in Christ* is not our natural state or condition. Our sinful nature has separated us from Christ, "but now *in Christ Jesus* ye who sometimes were far off are made nigh by the blood of Christ" (Eph 2:13). This change has produced a new heart and a new life with new desires and aims. "If any man be *in Christ,* he is a new creature" (2 Cor. 5:17). New life is naturally weak. Paul writes to the Corinthian Christians: "I, brethren, could not speak unto you as spiritual, but as unto carnal, even as unto babes *in Christ*" (1 Cor. 3:1). Growth requires proper nourishment. "As newborn babes, desire the sincere milk of the Word, that ye may grow thereby" (1 Peter 2:2). But weak or strong, "ye are all the children of God by faith *in Christ Jesus*" (Gal. 3:26), whether Jews or Gentiles. "The Gentiles should be fellowheirs, and of the same body, and partakers of His promise *in Christ* by the Gospel" (Eph. 3:6). "Ye are all one *in Christ Jesus*" (Gal. 3:28). "We, being many, are one body *in Christ,* and everyone members one of another" (Rom. 12:5).

Because we have redemption through His blood (Eph. 1:7), "there is therefore no condemnation to them which are *in Christ Jesus*" (Rom. 8:1).

Our high calling *in Christ* (Phil. 3:14) calls for our response, "for we are His workmanship, created *in Christ Jesus* unto good works" (Eph. 2:10). Our daily conduct requires that "as ye have therefore, received Christ Jesus, the Lord, so walk ye *in Him*" (Col. 2:6).

"Likewise reckon ye also yourselves to be dead indeed unto sin, but alive unto God *through Jesus Christ* our Lord" (Rom. 6:11).

Life *in Christ* is not all ease and leisure. Attacks will be made and there are battles to be fought, therefore, "Stand fast *in the Lord,* my dearly beloved" (Phil. 4:1). For some there may even be prison, as experienced by Paul in Rome: "My bonds *in Christ* are manifest in all the palace" (Phil. 1:13). But in all adversity the Christian will find an abundant source of divine help, which enables him to say, "I can do all things through Christ which strengthened me" (Phil. 4:13). No matter how great the hardships, we can confidently and joyfully say with Paul: "Thanks be unto God, which always causeth us to triumph *in Christ*" (2 Cor. 2:14). We can even meet death triumphantly for *in Christ* we share His victory over it. And when life's little day draws to its close, the believer who has lived *in Christ* will also fall asleep *in Him* to await the resurrection when he shall be with Him forevermore, for "them also which sleep *in Jesus* will God bring with Him" (1 Thess. 4:14).

> My soul's best Friend, how well contented
> Am I, reposing on Thy breast;
> By sin no more am I tormented
> Since Thou dost grant me peace and rest.
> Oh, may the grace that Thou hast given
> For me a foretaste be of heaven,
> Where I shall bask in joys divine!
> Away, vain world, with fleeting pleasures;
> In Christ I have abiding treasures.
> Oh, comfort sweet, my Friend is mine!

Jesus, King Most Wonderful

Behold, thy King cometh unto thee.

Zech. 9:9

Pilate therefore said unto Him, Art Thou a king then? Jesus answered, Thou sayest that I am a king. To this end was I born, and for this cause came I into the world, that I should bear witness unto the truth. Everyone that is of the truth heareth My voice.

John 18:37

Among the various descriptive titles assigned to the Savior was that of a king. This implied authority, power, and concern for the welfare of His subjects.

Long before Pilate inquired about the kingship of Jesus the Old Testament prophets were proclaiming royal descent and honor for the Messiah, and more than five centuries before, Zechariah identified Him as king when he foretold Christ's dramatic entry into Jerusalem on Palm Sunday. "Rejoice greatly, O daughter of Zion; shout, O daughter of Jerusalem: behold, thy King cometh unto thee: He is just, and having salvation" (Zech. 9:9).

The great majority of the people misunderstood the promises of a Messianic king and His kingdom, and were looking for an earthly ruler who would display wealth, pomp, and power, and whose citizens could be counted in a national census. There were but few who perceived the true kingly nature of the meek and lowly Jesus. One was Nathanael who declared: "Rabbi, Thou art the Son of God: Thou art the king of Israel" (John 1:49). Another was His companion on the cross who pleaded, "Lord, remember me when Thou comest into Thy kingdom" (Luke 23:42).

Jesus tried to correct these misconceptions and told

the Pharisees: "The kingdom of God cometh not with observation: neither shall they say, Lo here! or, lo there! for, behold, the kingdom of God is within you" (Luke 17:20-21).

Jesus desired only to be a spiritual king and was rejected as such by Israel. When the people tried to make Him their earthly king after His miraculous feeding of the multitude, He would have no part of it, and He left them to be by Himself (John 6:15). Yet when His enemies were required by Pilate to bring a charge against Jesus before he would accept Him for trial, the accusation they brought was that He made Himself a king.

It did not take Pilate long to see that Jesus had no ambition to be a rival to Tiberius or to start a rebellion. When the puzzled governor asked, "What hast Thou done?" Jesus answered, "My kingdom is not of this world" (John 18:35-36). We thank God for that. If His kingdom had been of this world, its glory would long since have faded with that of the Roman Empire.

Jesus is a king indeed; His claim is legitimate. "To this end was I born." He had not usurped His kingship from another, nor acquired it by conquest. His right to rule in our hearts cannot be denied, yet He forces Himself on no one. He rules by love alone and His subjects are all who are faithful to His Word. It was a fatal mistake for the crowd to tell Pilate: "We have no king but Caesar" (John 19:15). They were renouncing any part in the vast kingdom of the Kings of kings and Lord of lords embracing all heaven and earth.

Before Jesus ascended the throne of the cross for the final act of His redemption of mankind from sin and death, He endured the cruel mockery of His kingship by the Roman soldiers. They amused themselves by subjecting Him to a mock coronation. With a coarse sense of humor they fitted Him out with a ludicrous imitation of royal attire. They found an old robe to serve their purpose. And what could be more ridiculous than a crown of thorns for His head? To complete their caricature of kingship they thrust a fragile reed into His right hand for a mock scepter. Now they were ready for their scornful mock adoration and vulgar abuse. "They bowed the knee before Him, and mocked Him, saying 'Hail, King of the Jews!' And they spit upon Him, and took the reed, and smote Him on the head" (Matt. 27:29-30). To all this Jesus responded with truly royal dignity befitting the King of kings.

For me, that I might be His own, now and forever!

> O Jesus, King most wonderful,
> Thou Conqueror renowned,
> Thou Sweetness most ineffable,
> In whom all joys are found!
>
> When once Thou visitest the heart,
> Then truth begins to shine,
> Then earthly vanities depart,
> Then kindles love divine.
>
> O Jesus, Light of all below,
> Thou Fount of life and fire,
> Surpassing all the joys we know,
> All that we can desire.
>
> May every heart confess Thy name
> And ever Thee adore
> And seeking Thee, itself inflame
> To seek Thee more and more.
>
> Thee may our tongues forever bless,
> Thee may we love alone,
> And ever in our lives express
> The image of Thine own.

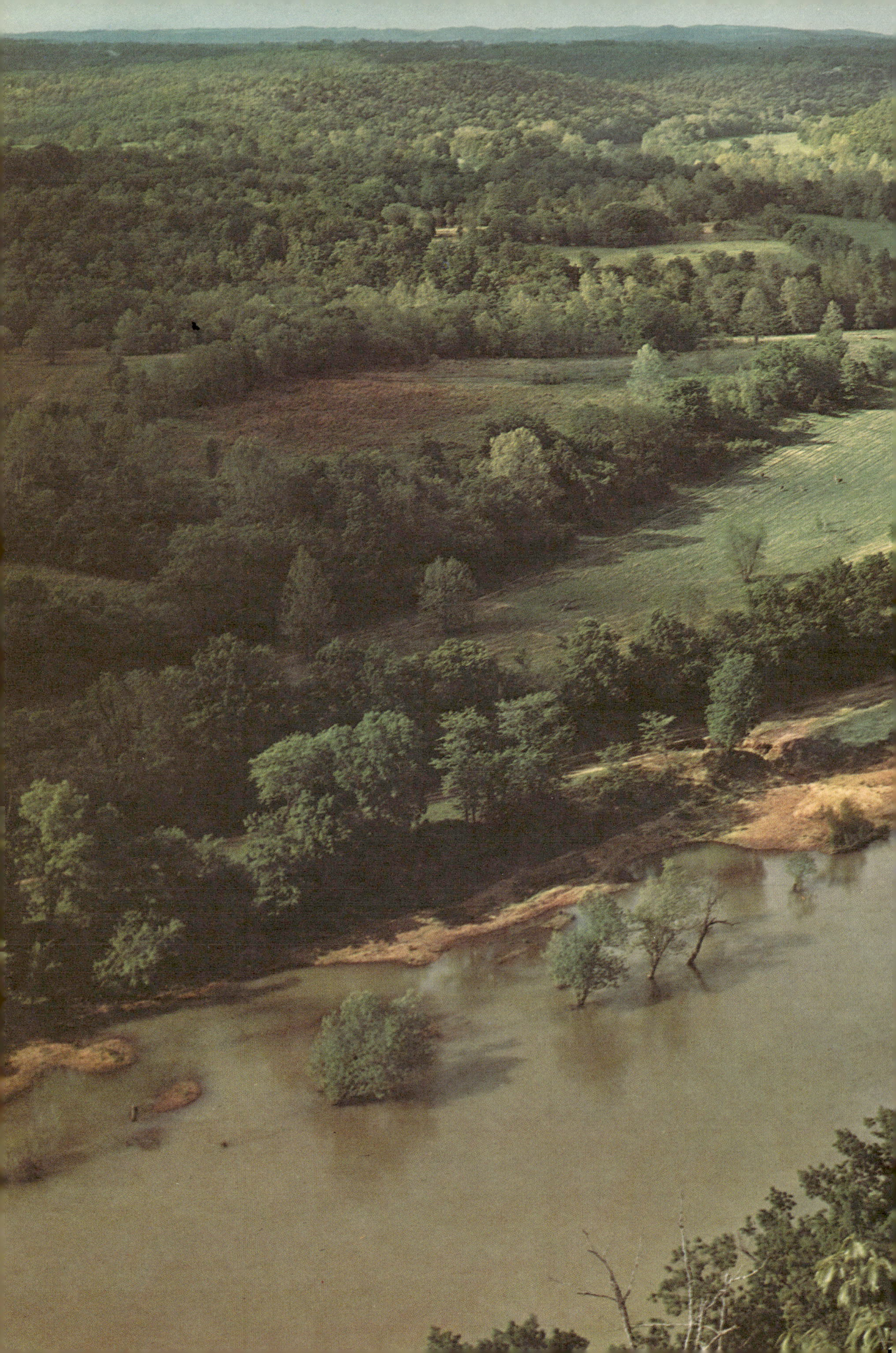

The Wondrous Cross

God forbid that I should glory, save in the cross of our Lord Jesus Christ.

Gal. 6:14

> When I survey the wondrous cross
> On which the Prince of Glory died,
> My richest gain I count but loss
> And pour contempt on all my pride.
>
> Forbid it, Lord, that I should boast
> Save in the death of Christ, my God
> All the vain things that charm me most,
> I sacrifice them to His blood.

The cross was once the symbol of suffering and shame, used as an instrument of torture for the execution of vicious criminals. That it has now become an emblem of victory and triumph that is proudly worn by countless Christians around the globe is a most remarkable transformation, brought about by the sacrificial death of the Son of God on Calvary's cross. By His immeasurable love of giving Himself as the ultimate sin offering for the redemption of a lost and condemned mankind, Jesus has hallowed the cross and transformed it into a *wondrous cross*.

Basically, the cross of Christ was no different from those of the two malefactors who were crucified with Him, or for that matter, all others that have been used for this cruel form of execution. It had no beauty, no glory, no attractiveness. It was an object feared and shunned. What set this cross apart from all other crosses was the person who hung upon it. The Savior's suffering and death upon the cross hallowed it and made it the supreme symbol of the love of God.

While there were many who looked upon crucifixion as evidence of deserved punishment and as a reflection on the character of the victim, the apostles did not try to play down or hide the historical fact of the cross, but instead freely stressed it in their preaching. So Paul wrote to the Corinthian Christians: "The preaching of the cross is to them that perish foolishness; but unto us which are saved it is the power of God. ... But we preach Christ crucified, unto the Jews a stumblingblock, and unto the Greeks foolishness; but unto them which are called, both Jews and Greeks, Christ the power of God, and the wisdom of God" (1 Cor. 1:18, 23, 24).

Jesus foretold the power of the cross when speaking of His imminent death. "I, if I be lifted up from the earth, will draw all men unto Me" (John 12:32). The first one drawn to the uplifted Jesus was His companion on the cross who turned to Him with the plea: "Lord, remember me when Thou comest into Thy kingdom," and received the glorious promise: "Verily I say unto thee, today shalt thou be with Me in Paradise" (Luke 23:42-43). Following him, there was a never-ending stream who join the Roman centurion under the cross in confessing: "Certainly this was a righteous man. Truly this was the Son of God" (Luke 23:47; Matt. 27:54).

By its great drawing power the cross of Christ has become an emblem of honor and a symbol of faith to all true believers, displayed on the altars of their churches and used to adorn their sanctuaries, as well as an article of personal adornment.

> Drawn to the cross, which Thou hast blest
> With healing gifts for souls distressed,
> To find in Thee my life, my rest,
> Christ Crucified, I come.
>
> Thou knowest all my griefs and fears,
> Thy grace abused, my misspent years;
> Yet now to Thee with contrite tears,
> Christ Crucified, I come.

Wash me and take away each stain;
Let nothing of my sin remain.
For cleansing, though it be through pain,
Christ Crucified, I come.

And then for work to do for Thee,
Which shall so sweet a service be
That angels well might envy me,
Christ Crucified, I come.

What Shall I Do with Jesus?

Pilate saith unto them, What shall I do then with Jesus which is called Christ?

Matt. 27:22

Historically this most important question was asked almost two thousand years ago by Pontius Pilate, Roman governor of the province of Judea, and the presiding judge at the civil trial of Jesus.

As governor and judge he had no business to ask it. It reflected cowardice on his part. He knew very well what he should do with Jesus, but he was too fainthearted to face up to his responsibility. He tried various ruses and schemes to avoid a verdict. His attempt to let the Jews settle their own problem failed when they told him: "It is not lawful for us to put any man to death" (John 18:31). The attempt to turn the case over to King Herod did not fare any better. Herod sent Jesus back to Pilate. Trying to be shrewd, Pilate then offered the people the opportunity to choose a prisoner to be freed at the Passover according to custom. The choice given them was between the popular Jesus, who just five days before, on Palm Sunday, had received a triumphant welcome on His entry into Jerusalem, and

Barabbas, a notorious criminal. This scheme backfired. Pilate was dumbfounded when they chose Barabbas. This evoked his puzzled question: "What shall I do then with Jesus"?

Properly so, the question was altogether personal. In spite of everything, he could not shift the responsibility or sidestep the decision. The final judgment in the case rested with him, and because he failed, his name lives on in infamy wherever Christians all around the world confess in the Apostle's Creed: "suffered under Pontius Pilate."

The question, What shall "*I*" do with Jesus? is by no means restricted to Pilate. No person who is confronted with Jesus can avoid answering it.

Six months earlier Jesus had impressed on His disciples that it was their personal attitude toward Him that counted. After listening to how others regarded Him, Jesus asked point-blank: "But whom say *ye* that I am?" (Matt. 16:15) Each of them would ultimately have to make a firm personal decision who He was. This would then also determine what to do with Him.

No one can remain indifferent toward Jesus, for He says, "He that is not with Me is against Me" (Matt. 12:30). No decision that we make can ever be more important than what to do with Jesus. This is perhaps brought out most forcibly when we reverse the question and ask ourselves, "What will Jesus do with me?" and then consider the alternative as He states it in (Matt. 10:32-33): "Whosoever therefore shall confess Me before men, him will I confess also before My Father which is in heaven. But whosoever shall deny Me before men, him will I also deny before My Father which is in heaven."

When we remember the boundless love of Jesus,

who first loved us and redeemed us with His innocent suffering and death and made us His own, we should respond with love and adoration, and gladly acknowledge Him as our Lord and Savior, and gratefully serve and obey Him, and boldly confess His name. Then life here will be more meaningful and life eternal our glorious prospect.

> Come, follow Me, the Savior spake,
> All in My way abiding;
> Deny yourselves, the world forsake,
> Obey My call and guiding.
> Oh, bear the cross, whate'er betide,
> Take My example for your guide.
>
> Then let us follow Christ, our Lord,
> And take the cross appointed
> And, firmly clinging to His Word,
> In suffering be undaunted.
> For who bears not the battle's strain
> The crown of life shall not obtain.

Open the Door

Behold, I stand at the door, and knock: if any man hear My voice, and open the door, I will come in to him, and will sup with him, and he with Me.

Rev. 3:20

Though first addressed to a congregation in Asia Minor, these words are intended also for you and for me. They were ordered written for all to read and to heed.

It is Christ Himself who is bringing a special message to the seven churches of Asia Minor through John, the beloved. He identifies Himself as "the Amen, the faithful and true witness, the beginning of the creation of God" (3:14).

Located in the wealthy city of Laodicea, this

congregation ranked first in earthly goods and boasted of its riches and self-sufficiency. However, the evaluation of Jesus was quite different. He put it last. While there were no false teachers or serious troublemakers, there was an absence of love and zeal for the Lord and His work, and there was no evidence of a living faith. They were neither hot nor cold, but lukewarm. They deserved to be disowned and rejected by Jesus. But in spite of their failings and shortcomings, He still loved them, and He follows His reproof and correction with some of the most tender and loving words to come from His lips.

"Behold", He says, to alert them that He was coming to them as their Friend and Savior, "I stand at the door and knock." He is seeking entrance into their hearts and lives to bring His priceless blessings to them. He is patiently standing and knocking with His hand and calling with His voice to gain attention of His presence.

In his masterful painting of the scene Holman Hunt has Jesus standing before a latchless door which can only be opened from within. What the artist wants to stress is that Jesus can be kept out of the hearts and lives of people by their indifference or unwillingness to let Him in.

Jesus, the Friend of sinners, stands at the door of every human heart and knocks, calls, and waits. He does not use force. He asks admission and waits for an invitation. The initiative is His. He comes to us, even as He told His disciples in the Upper Room: "Ye have not chosen Me, but I have chosen you" (John 15:16). He speaks to us through His sacred Word, both Law and Gospel, as well as by His daily kindness and favors.

He comes with the gracious promise: "if any man

hear My voice, and open the door, I will come in to him, and will sup with him, and he with Me." Whoever opens the door of his heart for Him to enter will be richly rewarded and blessed with the Savior's presence. A close and friendly fellowship and His indwelling will transform and renew it.

Are we ready and eager to open our hearts to the Guest who is knocking at the door, or are we too indifferent or too busy with many things and events to pay attention to Him? That would be tragic indeed, for to do nothing is to do the most dreadful thing possible. It is to keep the door shut in the face of Jesus. It means the rejection of one's salvation.

> Behold a Stranger at the door!
> He gently knocks, has knocked before,
> Has waited long, is waiting still;
> You treat no other friend so ill.
>
> But will He prove a friend indeed?
> He will; the very Friend you need;
> The Friend of sinners—yes, 'tis He,
> With garments dyed on Calvary.
>
> O lovely attitude! He stands
> With melting heart and laden hands;
> O matchless kindness! And He shows
> This matchless kindness to His foes.
>
> Admit Him lest His anger burn
> And He, departing, ne'er return;
> Admit Him, or the hour's at hand
> When at His door denied you'll stand.
>
> Oh, let the heavenly Stranger in,
> Let in thy heart His reign begin.
> Admit Him, open wide the door,
> And He will bless thee evermore.
>
> Enter now my waiting heart,
> Glorious King and Lord most holy.
> Dwell in me and ne'er depart,
> Though I am but poor and lowly.
> Ah, what riches will be mine
> When Thou art my Guest Divine!

Afar Off

Peter followed Jesus afar off . . . to see the end.

Matt. 26:58

Peter had been especially close to Jesus. He had won the Master's praise for his perceptive confession of Jesus as "the Christ, the Son of the living God" (Matt. 16:16). He was one of the select trio to accompany Jesus at the raising of Jairus' daughter, and again on the Mount of Transfiguration. He was chosen with John to make the preparations for the memorable Passover celebration, and to be with Jesus in the Garden of Gethsemane. He cherished that closeness.

But now Peter followed Jesus afar off. A sudden and dramatic change had taken place. A crisis had come into his life. The staunch confessor had become timid and fearful. The bold defender was keeping out of range in the shadows of the night.

Peter was offended because the Master meekly submitted to capture by the throng of armed soldiers, temple guard, and others who had come out against Him. He had even reprimanded Peter for his misguided zeal in rushing to the Master's defense with the sword.

The popular Jewish expectation was that the coming Messiah would restore the kingdom to Israel as in the days of King David. This expectation persisted among the disciples despite the Master's teaching about a totally different kingdom. Earlier in the evening, at the Passover celebration, the disciples had quarreled among themselves about rank and honor in this kingdom. The Master's lesson in humility by washing the disciples' feet had shamed them, but did not eliminate their misunderstanding, but the course of events this night shattered this hope of eminence and grandeur for Peter. It became apparent that Jesus was not going to act in this direction.

Peter was shaken. Forgetting his proud boast to die with Jesus rather than to take offense at Him, he fled with the rest. But before he had gone far, Peter halted in his flight. Was it a feeling of shame and guilt? Or was it curiosity? He turned about and followed afar off—"to see the end".

Following Jesus afar off is not the kind of following that He wants. It does not show Him the honor and devotion that is due unto Him. It is also dangerous for the follower. For Peter it was the first step of his shameful denial. For others it is the sign that loyalty to Him is weakening, and the danger of falling away from Him completely is very real.

When the distance between Jesus and His followers grows wider the fault is never with Him. He does not turn away from them or forsake them. He came into this world to seek and to save the lost. He invites the troubled and weary to come unto Him to find rest for their souls. He pleads with sinners to follow Him on the way that leads heavenward, and He promises to be with His own until the end of days. If Jesus is more remote from you than He once was, it is not because He has moved away from you, but you have moved away from Him.

Only seldom is the break with Jesus sudden and abrupt. This can happen when some new force or person enters into someone's life. Even then there is bound to have been some loosening of ties of love and devotion to Jesus. But most often it is a slow and gradual process, yielding little by little to the enticements and temptations that seem so inviting. Unless a halt is made in time, following Jesus afar off can end in losing Him completely, and losing Him, losing eternal life. What an unspeakable tragedy that would be!

May we never outgrow that precious prayer of childhood:

> Be near me, Lord Jesus!
> I ask Thee to stay
> Close by me forever
> And love me, I pray.
> Bless all the dear children
> In Thy tender care
> And take me to heaven
> To live with Thee there. Amen.

When anything begins to drive a wedge between us and Jesus it is time to stop and seriously reflect about the dangerous consequences that will follow and to ask for divine help in prayer.

> O God, forsake me not!
> Lord, hear my supplication!
> In every evil hour
> Help me o'ercome temptation;
> And when the prince of hell
> My conscience seeks to blot,
> Be Thou not far from me—
> O God, forsake me not!

One of Them

Surely thou art one of them.

Mark 14:70

These words were spoken in a tone of disparagement. They implied something evil and sinister. "One of them" meant a disciple of this Jesus of Nazareth, who was brought into the palace of the High Priest Caiaphas for trial before the Jewish High Court. In the hostile atmosphere present, being identified with Him was not only regarded a reflection on a person, but might also be dangerous.

Peter sensed this. When Jesus permitted Himself to be taken prisoner at Gethsemane, He still exercised His authority and demanded safety for His disciples, but by following into the territory of the enemy, Peter had placed himself into jeopardy. Something about him aroused suspicion, and led to the accusation: "Surely thou art one of them".

There was a time, and, thank God, would be again, when Peter was proud to be "one of them," but at this moment fear swept him off his feet, and he vehemently denied any connection with the captive Jesus.

Are you one of them? is a question that keeps echoing down through the ages and touches the lives of all disciples of Jesus. Not seldom is it asked in situations where it is unpopular, even if not dangerous, to confess allegiance. Fear of being ridiculed or shunned can then easily make them cringe and lead to a denial of Jesus, either vocally as Peter did, or by silencing the lips.

Well for us if we can courageously and confidently declare that we are indeed "one of them," for Jesus solemnly declares: "Whosoever therefore shall confess Me before men, him will I confess also before My Father which is in heaven. But whosoever shall deny Me before men, him will I also deny before My Father which is in heaven" (Matt. 10:32-33).

When the great day comes when we must all stand before God in judgment, the witness of Jesus will determine our eternal destiny. Then the decisive factor in our favor will be that He can point to us and say: "Father, this My brother, My sister, has confessed Me before men and I acknowledge this person as Mine own." For such there awaits the gracious invitation to eternal bliss and joy with our Lord and Savior, together with all His saints and angels, in the heavenly mansions. But woe to those who have not confessed Him before men, for He will be compelled to deny them before the Father in heaven. Jesus will not be with anyone there who has not been with Him here.

What an unspeakable blessing to belong to the number of those who are acknowledged by Jesus as being one of His own! What an honor! There is none greater that mortal man could ever aspire to.

> Jesus! and shall it ever be,
> A mortal man ashamed of Thee?
> Ashamed of Thee, whom angels praise,
> Whose glories shine through endless days?
>
> Ashamed of Jesus? Sooner far
> Let evening blush to own a star.
> He sheds the beams of light divine
> O'er this benighted soul of mine.
>
> Ashamed of Jesus? Just as soon
> Let midnight be ashamed of noon.
> 'Tis midnight with my soul till He,
> Bright Morning Star, bids darkness flee.
>
> Ashamed of Jesus, that dear Friend
> On whom my hopes of heav'n depend?
> No; when I blush, be this my shame,
> That I no more revere His name.
>
> Ashamed of Jesus? Yes I may
> When I've no guilt to wash away,
> No tear to wipe, no good to crave,
> No fear to quell, no soul to save.
>
> Till then—nor is my boasting vain—
> Till than I boast a Savior slain;
> And oh, my this my glory be,
> That Christ is not ashamed of me!

Jesus Loved Him

Jesus wept. Then said the Jews, Behold how He loved him.
John 11:35-36

Three times we are told that Jesus loved Lazarus, the brother of Mary and Martha, without even hinting at a single cause or reason on his part to evoke it. Not one spoken word of his is recorded. In fact, we don't even know whether he was able to speak or not. Not one deed or action of his is recorded, save that he came forth from the tomb at the command of Jesus, and that he was present at the banquet with Jesus. No mention is made of anything he did. We only read of what others said about him and did for him. But Jesus loved him warmly and deeply.

It is a picture of love totally unselfish and immaculately pure. But then, is not this the way God's love always is? Undeserving and unworthy as we all are in the sight of the holy and righteous God, He still loves us with a fervent and abiding love.

We choose to think of Lazarus as representative of those deeply in need of help, and service, and loving care, and compassion; people whom God has placed among us to help, care for, support, and love for Jesus' sake.

Some primitive tribes have operated under the rule of getting rid of those who could not work and produce. This heathen spirit has raised its sinister head also among certain "civilized" people, who have adopted the notion that the world would be better off without the many infirm and helpless people. They begrudge them all the care, time, service, and money expended on them. They are wrong. The world would not be better off without them. The world would be infinitely poorer without the helpless and the needy.

What a cold and heartless place this world would become if there were no need and no opportunity to exercise love and compassion. Since sin has made mankind naturally selfish and heartless, we have constant need of opportunity and encouragement to exercise the godly virtues of unselfish love and compassion. The opportunity to exercise our love, and to help it to grow more pure, more noble, more rich, and more Christlike is provided in the persons of special need whom the Lord has placed at our doors or into our homes. The encouragement is given by the example of Jesus and by His instruction. He declares: "A new commandment I give unto you, That ye love one another; as I have loved you, that ye also love one another" (John 13:34). And St. Paul encourages us: "Bear ye one another's burdens, and so fulfill the law of Christ" (Gal. 6:2).

>   Jesus, Thy boundless love to me
>   No thought can reach, no tongue declare;
>   Unite my thankful heart with Thee
>   And reign without a rival there.
>   To Thee alone, dear Lord, I live;
>   Myself to Thee, dear Lord, I give.
>
>   Oh, grant that nothing in my soul
>   May dwell but Thy pure love alone!
>   Oh, may Thy love possess me whole,
>   My Joy, my Treasure, and my Crown!
>   All coldness from my heart remove;
>   My ev'ry act, word, thought be love.

He Touched Him

Behold, there came a leper and worshiped Him, saying, Lord, if Thou wilt, Thou canst make me clean. And Jesus put forth His hand, and touched him, saying, I will; be thou clean. And immediately his leprosy was cleansed.

Matt. 8:2-3

Jesus touched the leper. That seems like a small and insignificant gesture. But for the leper it was an act of vital importance. Not that his being healed depended on being touched by the Lord. Jesus healed others by His all-powerful Word, without any physical contact, but by stepping forward and stretching out His hand and touching the leper, He was responding to the man's deep inner need. St. Luke tells us that he was "full of leprosy." His case was far advanced, hopelessly incurable. For a long time he had been isolated by his loathsome disease from family, friends, and relatives. He could only see people from a safe distance. How he must have yearned for just the touch of a hand. But he was forbidden to come near a well person, and they were forbidden to come near him.

But Jesus, understanding the intense desire in the heart of this man, does not shrink from contact with him. He reaches across the wall of separation and touches him as He exercises His healing power. This simple gesture by Jesus tells more than words can convey of His compassionate love and tenderness for those in need.

There were other times in the ministry of Jesus when He expressed genuine human feeling by the touch of His hand, as in healing the deaf-mute (Mark 7:33), giving sight to the blind (Matt. 20:34), and placing His hands in blessing upon the little children (Mark 10:13).

We know, of course, that Jesus still has the power and compassion to help in time of need, but there is also a deeper meaning that His sympathetic response to the plea of the leprous outcast reveals to us. It shows that Jesus understands the individual, personal needs of people and responds to them in accordance with their best interest. He also knows and understands our own special problems and what is best for us under the circumstances. And while we are not privileged to have Jesus step up to us and touch us physically, as He did for the leper, because He has withdrawn His visible presence from the earth through His ascension into heaven, we know that He is constantly near us with His unseen presence, allowing us in faith to put our hand in His for support and guidance.

If we would be like Jesus, we dare not shrink from touching the lonely, and neglected, and social outcasts. There must be in our hearts the loving, compassionate, understanding concern for the suffering and distressed, and a readiness to give comfort and support to them. We can often lift their spirits and brighten their day with a firm handclasp, a sincere pat on the back, or a friendly arm around them, as we listen to their problems or offer help and express concern. Indeed, the touch of Jesus is a splendid pattern for us to follow.

> Let us ever walk with Jesus.
> Follow His example pure,
> Flee the world, which would deceive us
> And to sin our souls allure.
> Ever in His footsteps treading,
> Body here, yet soul above,
> Full of faith and hope and love,
> Let us do the Father's bidding.
> Faithful Lord, abide with me;
> Savior, lead, I follow Thee.

For Me

The Son of God . . . loved me and gave Himself for me.
Gal. 2:20

In these few words St. Paul summarizes the profound teachings of the Christian's righteousness before God, and focuses it directly on the individual person. The firm conviction that Paul felt and expressed here, applies to each and every child of God, for "God... spared not His own Son, but delivered Him up for us all" (Rom. 8:31-32), not for a vague, nameless mass of humanity, but for every single one who by faith has become a member of the family of God. For you and for me.

He gave Himself *for* me—not only in my behalf, not only for my benefit, but *in my stead.* He took my place. He became my *Substitute.*

He, the only begotten Son of God, gave Himself for me, a poor sinful being, so small and insignificant in this great universe. For me He offered Himself as a sacrifice on Calvary's cross. Nobody took His life. He laid it down. "Therefore doth My Father love Me, because I lay down My life, that I might take it again. No man taketh it from Me, but I lay it down of Myself. I have power to lay it down, and I have power to take it again" (John 10:17-18). He gave Himself.

There was nothing in me to compel Him to do this for Me. He was moved by His own boundless love. "He loved me, and gave Himself for me." Such love is beyond compare, for "when we were enemies, we were reconciled to God by the death of His Son" (Rom. 5:10). That love gives His sacrifice its wondrous value.

This sacrificial love of Christ means more to me

than anything else ever can. It means that all my sins have been blotted out and will be remembered no more. It means peace with God, here in this life, and the full assurance of eternal life in the Father's house. It echoes the message of Isaiah: "He endured the suffering that should have been ours, the pain that we should have borne. All the while we thought that His suffering was punishment sent by God. But because of our sins He was wounded, beaten because of the evil we did. We are healed by the punishment He suffered, made whole by the blows He received" (53:4-5 TEV).

"For ME" persuades me to apply the sacrifice of Christ to myself. Because of it God sees only the righteousness of Christ in me, and salvation is now and forever my personal possession.

My response to His marvelous love must be to love Him and to live unto Him. "He died for all, that they which live should not henceforth live unto themselves, but unto Him which died for them and rose again" '2 Cor. 5:15).

> Thy life was giv'n for me:
> Thy blood, O Lord, was shed,
> That I might ransomed be,
> And quickened from the dead.
> Thy life was giv'n for me:
> What have I giv'n for Thee?
>
> Oh, let my life be given,
> My years for Thee be spent,
> World's fetters all be riven,
> And pain with joy be blent!
> Thou gavest Thyself for me;
> I give myself to Thee.

Not Ashamed of Us

These all died in faith, not having received the promises, but having seen them afar off, and were persuaded of them, and embraced them, and confessed that they were strangers and pilgrims on the earth. For they that say such things declare plainly that they seek a country. And truly, if they had been mindful of that country from whence they came out, they might have had opportunity to have returned. But now they desire a better country, that is, an heavenly; Wherefore God is not ashamed to be called their God; for He hath prepared for them a city.

Heb. 11:13-16.

What a startling statement, "wherefore God is not ashamed to be called their God!" Knowing human foibles and frailties, perverseness and disobedience, one must marvel that there should be anyone in the human race of whom God would not have reason enough, and more, to be deeply ashamed. Of whom, then, is this remarkable statement made?

In the first instance, they were those heroes of faith whose names are mentioned in that great chapter of faith from which this statement is taken. They were Enoch and Abel, Noah, Abraham and Sarah, Isaac and Jacob, Joseph and Moses, and others. God was pleased to be known before mankind as their God.

Not because they possessed spotless characters was God not ashamed of them, for they too were sinners like all others. but there were three things these people had in common that made them acceptable to the Lord, their God. (1) They were persuaded of God's promises. (2) They embraced them. (3) They confessed that they were strangers and pilgrims on the earth.

God had given many promises to His people: His divine presence and help in time of need and danger; bread without scarcity in the Land of Promise, as well as

51

many other temporal blessings; but the greatest and noblest of God's promises centered in the Redeemer, the Saviour from sin, our Lord Jesus Christ. Though none of these people lived to see the fulfillment of these promises regarding the Savior, they were nevertheless persuaded of them. They judged God, who had made these promises, faithful and believed them.

Furthermore, their faith was not a mere acknowledgement of the truthfulness and trustworthiness of the promises, but a personal acceptance of them, for they embraced these promises. They rested their hope and confidence on them. They took this promised Redeemer, as yet afar off, into their hearts and relied on Him for their salvation.

And finally, we are told, "they confessed that they were strangers and pilgrims on the earth." To them the earth with its pleasures and treasures was not the purpose and goal of their existence, but a stopping place on the journey to the real home of God's people, the heavenly mansions above.

By thus specifying the reasons why God was not ashamed of these people of old, the inspired writer invites us to follow their example and partake of their blessings. We have an even greater reason than they had to be persuaded of the promises of God and to embrace them, for we have the good fortune to live in an age when all the promises concerning the Savior have been fulfilled, from the least to the greatest

> What the fathers most desired,
> What the prophets' heart inspired,
> What they longed for many a year,
> Stands fulfilled in glory here.

We do not have any more reason for looking upon the earth as the ultimate goal of our existence than did

Abraham or Moses. Modern science has given us many marvelous things and conveniences that were unknown to them, but the basic problems that they had are still the same with us. Fear still stalks through the land, and death still separates people from all earthly things and associations. Sin has blighted the earth, and its fatal germ has infected all mankind. Only in the mansions of the Father's house above will our soul find lasting peace and perfect rest. Indeed, we are strangers here, and heaven is our home.

How inexpressibly wonderful, then, to have the blessed assurance that God is not ashamed to be called our God if we will follow the pattern of faith here set before us. With faith in our hearts, and our eyes fixed upon heaven, the allurements of earth seem small and insignificant in comparison with the knowledge that God is not ashamed of us.

> A pilgrim and a stranger,
> I journey here below;
> Far distant is my country
> The home to which I go.
> Here I must toil and travail,
> Oft weary and opprest;
> But there my God shall lead me
> To everlasting rest.
>
> There I shall dwell forever,
> No more a parting guest,
> With all Thy blood-bought children
> In everlasting rest,
> The pilgrim toils forgotten,
> The pilgrim conflicts o'er,
> All earthly griefs behind me,
> Eternal joys before.

The Common People

The common people heard Him glady.

Mark 12:37

St Mark makes a very significant observation concerning the response of the people to the person and teaching of Christ. After pointing out the hostility and faultfinding of the Jewish leaders toward Him, he adds the terse comment, "The common people heard Him gladly."

It was that memorable Tuesday between Palm Sunday and Good Friday, the last full working day of our Lord's public ministry. After His talks with His disciples on the way from Bethany to Jerusalem, He visited the Temple for the last time. Scarcely had He entered the sacred courts and begun to teach, when He was met by an official delegation of chief priests, scribes, and elders, who challenged His authority and demanded an accounting. They were quickly silenced, and Jesus went on with His teaching in which He covered a wide variety of subjects, including denunciations of the hypocrisy of the scribes and Pharisees, and His lament over the fate of Jerusalem.

While the people of position and distinction were, for the most part, hostile toward Jesus and His message, the rank and file, whom Mark called the common people, were friendly and listened to Him with great interest.

In addition to the regular citizens of Jerusalem, who lived and worked within its walls, and showed their love for God's house by regular and faithful worship in the temple, there were also large numbers of festive pilgrims present who had come to the the Holy City to celebrate the passover festival. All classes of faithful Israelites from far and near were represented. Most of them were "common people," people who worked with their hands, gardeners, carpenters and fishermen, servants and maids, tradesmen and shopkeepers, shepherds, and others. These common people, with an open heart for God's message, and an open mind toward Jesus, filled the spacious temple courts and listened to the masterful Teacher with eagerness. They heard Him gladly.

The pattern was familiar. It happened over and over during the course of His public ministry—hostility from the leaders and hearty joyful acceptance by the common people.

When Jesus returned home to Capernaum from a very busy preaching tour on the other side of the Sea of Galilee, He received a very cordial welcome from the common people. They had learned to know and love Jesus. They had heard the sweet message of God's love and salvation from His lips. They had seen His mighty works. They were glad to have such a wonderful Friend among them once more.

It was the common people from far and wide who gathered around Him at the mountain to listen to His matchless sermon. It was the common people who followed Him by the thousands into the wilderness to be fed by Him with the barley loaves and fishes as well as the bread of life. They all heard Him gladly because He taught the will of God plainly without fear or favor.

It was the common people who made up most of the festive throng that welcomed Jesus with jubilant Hosannas and palm branches on His entry into Jerusalem just two days before, and the common children who continued the Hosannas in the temple courts on Monday. Both displays of adoration were sharply condemned by the Jewish leaders.

There were, indeed, some among the rich and

influential who also listened to Jesus and became His followers, like Nicodemus and Joseph of Arimathaea, members of the Council, Zacchaeus, the tax collector, the Roman centurion on Calvary, and others unnamed, who confessed Jesus as Lord and God, but these were exceptions.

The story was much the same after Pentecost. While we read of the Ethiopian official who believed and was baptized, and of a great many priests who accepted the faith (Acts 6:7), the rapid growth of the New Testament Church came from the ranks of the common people.

It was no different when the Gospel was carried out into the world by the believers who were scattered by persecution, and by the apostles and their co-workers. The pattern was much the same as in the Corinthian congregation. "For ye see your calling, brethren, how that not many wise men after the flesh, not many mighty, not many noble, are called: but God hath chosen the foolish things of the world to confound the wise; and God hath chosen the weak things of the world to confound the things which are mighty; and base things of the world, and things which are despised, hath God chosen, yea, and things which are not, to bring to nought things that are: that no flesh should glory in His presence" (1 Cor. 1:26-29).

Since then, down through the centuries, unnumbered multitudes from all walks of life, including royalty and nobility, have been drawn to Christ crucified, and have confessed and followed Him, but it was always the common people who filled the ranks of the "Christian soldiers." So even today, the strength and success of the church does not rest in people of distinction and influence in the affairs of this world, but in the mighty host of the common people who with humble hearts gladly hear the message of life and salvation proclaimed by our Lord through His faithful servants. The precious Gospel of Christ will bless all, the rich and mighty as well as the poor and lowly, if they will only come to their Savior with contrite hearts and childlike faith.

> We are His people, we his care,
> Our souls and all our mortal frame.
> What lasting honors shall we rear,
> Almighty Maker, to Thy name?
>
> We'll crowd Thy gates with joyful songs,
> High as the heavens our voices raise;
> And earth, with her ten thousand tongues,
> Shall fill Thy courts with sounding praise.

What a Wonderful God!

O the depth of the riches both of the wisdom and knowledge of God! How unserarchable are His judgments, and His ways past finding out! . . . For of Him, and through Him, and to Him, are all things: to whom be glory for ever. Amen.
Rom. 11:33, 36

The marvelous strides made by mankind in many areas of science and knowledge in recent years have caused many to glorify human accomplishment, and to either ignore God completely, or to underestimate Him and to lose a feeling of awe and reverence for Him. That is tragic wherever it happens. God cannot be eliminated from His supreme authority in the universe, nor can He be measured by any human yardstick.

St. Paul gives us a much nobler picture of God. He was completely overwhelmed by His greatness and exclaims in profound admiration: "O the depth of the riches both of the wisdom and knowledge of God!"

This supreme wisdom and knowledge manifested itself in many ways and places. It is first of all apparent in His works of creation. The whole universe bears witness to the creative genius of God. Look at the starry skies and probe into outer space and marvel at the multitude of the heavenly bodies and the precision with which they move on their courses. Truly, "The heavens declare the glory of God; and the firmament showeth His handiwork" (Ps. 19:1). Look round about us in the world in which we dwell and behold the wonders of nature on every hand. How prolific the plant and animal life found in such astounding variety and beauty! Look through the microscope and marvel at the structure and complexity of a tiny living cell.

No less does the wisdom and knowledge of God show itself in the preservation and maintenance of all that He has made. Behold how life in its various forms is reproduced and sustained by the constant multiplying of the food supply. Jesus reminds us that not one sparrow falls to the ground without the Father's consent (Matt. 10:29). How much greater, then, is His care and loving concern for us, who were created in His own image, and endowed with immortal souls.

In all these ways we have striking evidence of the incomparable wisdom and knowledge of God. Truly, "the fool hath said in his heart, There is no God" (Ps. 14:1).

But where we must really stand in awe and wonder is when we contemplate God's plan of salvation for us. Ever since sin came into this world, to destroy the perfect relationship between God and man, restoring that relationship has been the basic problem. All human efforts have fallen far short because they were based on man's effort and achievement to gain the favor of God and appease His anger. In His wisdom and knowledge God Himself prepared a way back into blessed fellowship with Him by sending His own Son to pay the penalty for our sins and to ransom us from the powers of darkness. Faith alone is required to receive full pardon and to be welcomed back into the heavenly Father's arms. Indeed, what a wonderful God! Of Him, and through Him, and to Him, are all things: to whom be glory forever. Amen.

> When all Thy mercies, O my God,
> My rising soul surveys,
> Transported with the view, I'm lost
> In wonder, love, and praise.

Walking with God

Enoch walked with God: and he was not; for God took him.
                                                    Gen. 5:24

> Savior, I long to walk
> Closer with Thee;
> Led by Thy guiding hand,
> Ever to be
> Constantly near Thy side,
> Quickened and purified,
> Living for Him who died
> Freely for me.

The ultimate in security is found in walking with God. When people conform their life and conduct to the divine will, they will experience the nearness of His presence and the feeling of complete safety.

Enoch, the seventh from Adam in the line of the ancestors of Jesus, is noted in the sacred Scriptures for walking with God. Living at a time when "the wickedness of man was great in the earth, and ... every imagination of the thoughts of his heart was only evil continually" (Gen. 6:5), Enoch found favor with God by his God-fearing behavior and witness and was counted among the great heroes of faith of the Old Testament. He was acknowledged by God to have pleased Him and received the very special reward of being spared from death.

Walking with God affords protection and safety. There is no reason to fear when the power of the Almighty is with us. Then we exult with Paul: "If God be for us, who can be against us?" (Rom. 8:31)

In his beloved Shepherd Psalm, David says: "Yea, though I walk through the valley of the shadow of death, I will fear no evil: for Thou art with me; Thy rod and Thy staff they comfort me" (Ps. 23:4). There was no need for him to run in fear as long as he knew that God was with him. No matter how near or how great the danger that was lurking in the shadows, he could walk calmly and fearlessly under His safety and protection.

Why should people run in fear when they have the promise of the abiding presence of Christ? Did He not say: "Lo, I am with you alway, even unto the end of the world"? (Matt. 28:20). They can walk with Him leisurely, confidently, safely on the way through life, unto life everlasting. He guides them by His Word. At His side they are secure.

Through His prophet Amos (3:3) the Lord asked: "Can two walk together, except they be agreed?" Walking with God means keeping step with Him and following where He leads. It means walking the way of His commandments. It excludes dashing ahead of Him or lagging behind Him; rushing hither and yon: doing things one's own way without heeding His direction or guidance.

Wilfully choosing one's own way is not walking with God, but apart from Him. Yet even children of God will sometimes do this. Peter was inclined to be impetuous and act without waiting for direction or answer from the Lord. But when he went his own way he invariably got into trouble. That is the danger when people become careless in their course of action.

It was not popular for Enoch to walk with God when he was surrounded by so much evil, and it is not popular or easy to do so today when there are so many distractions and temptations that hinder a person from doing so. It takes determination to follow the directions that the Lord gives us in His Word, and it means letting Him lead us by the hand. Only then will we be able to walk with God.

> Jesus only can impart
> Balm to heal the smitten heart;
> Peace that flows from sins forgiv'n,
> Joy that lifts the soul to heav'n;
> Faith and hope to walk with God
> In the way that Enoch trod.
>
> O my Savior, help afford
> By Thy Spirit and Thy Word!
> When my wayward heart would stray,
> Keep me in the narrow way;
> Grace in time of need supply
> While I live and when I die.

Glorify God

Ye are bought with a price; therefore glorify God in your body and in your spirit, which are God's.

1 Cor. 6:20

As Jesus passed through the land, teaching wherever He went and proving His divine authority by performing His mighty miracles—healing the man with palsy; raising the son of the widow of Nain from the dead; cleansing the lepers; restoring sight to the blind; and others—we read again and again that the people glorified Him and God. By their spontaneous praise they were acclaiming Him as a teacher sent from God and were fulfilling one of the fore-most functions of God's beneficiaries, glorifying God.

In the Old Testament God said: "Call upon Me in the day of trouble: I will deliver thee, and thou shalt glorify Me" (Ps. 50:15). When the people were negligent in their worship, and put off rebuilding the temple after their return from captivity, God commanded: "Build the house; and I will take pleasure in it, and I will be glorified" (Hag. 1:8). In the New Testament He spoke through the apostle Paul to the Corinthian Christians and to us: "Ye are bought with a price; therefore glorify God in your body and in your spirit, which are God's."

We see then that it is God's holy will that we should glorify Him. And there is good and sound reason why we should do this. We belong to God. We are His not only through creation, but especially by redemption. When some like to say that their life is their own, and they can do with it as they please, they lose sight of the fact that they have been dearly bought, not with perishable things like gold and silver, but with the holy precious blood of Christ and with His innocent suffering and death and therefore are not really their own after all. They now belong to God and for this reason it also becomes their duty to glorify God.

Such glorifying should be total, in body and spirit. The aim of all our activities and conduct should have God's glory in sight. "Whether therefore ye eat, or drink, or whatsoever ye do, do all to the glory of God" (1 Cor. 10:31). At work or play, business or handicraft, study or research, leisure or rest, public worship or private meditation, every use of the body and mind should contribute to glorifying God. In the Sermon on the Mount, Jesus taught: "Let your light so shine before men, that they may see your good works, and glorify your Father which is in heaven" (Matt. 5:16). The opportunity to glorify God often comes at unexpected times and circumstances. When the Roman centurion witnessed the events surrounding the death of Jesus on Calvary's cross "he glorified God, saying, Certainly this was a righteous man. Truly this was the Son of God" (Luke 23:47; Matt. 27:54).

We reflect our gratitude for the distinctive, God-given ability to worship and praise the Creator, when we glorify God. Let us then "give unto the Lord the glory due unto His name" (1 Chron. 16:29).

> All ye who on this earth do dwell,
> Give thanks and glorify
> The Lord whose praises ever swell
> In Seraph songs on high.
>
> Lift up your hearts in praise to God,
> Himself best Gift of all,
> Who works His wonders all abroad,
> Upholding great and small.
>
> Long as we tarry here below
> Our saving Health is He;
> And when from earth to heaven we go,
> May He our Portion be!

Sing to the Lord

I will sing to the Lord, because He has dealt bountifully with me.

Ps. 13:6 RSV

David declares his confidence that the Lord will not forget him in his need, but will again show his faithfulness and help him. In joyful gratitude he proclaims that he will sing to the Lord. As he had done so often, the Sweet Singer of Israel will once again praise his God in song.

The special talent to make and appreciate music, and especially to express one's innermost feelings in song, is truly one of the Creator's most precious gifts to mankind. It finds expression in many and varied situations in life, from the hilarity of festivity to the mournful lament of deep sorrow. But the noblest use for this gift is in glorifying God for His great goodness and love.

Like David, God's people throughout the ages have been moved to sing praise and thanksgiving to the Lord for His divine favor. The ecstacy of deliverance from the host of Pharaoh at the Red Sea rings out in the songs of Moses and Miriam (Ex. 15). The children of Israel sang praises to God as they traveled to the Promised Land (Num. 21:17-18). The women of Israel celebrated David's triumph over Goliath with jubilant singing to the accompaniment of musical instruments (1 Sam. 18:6-7). The annual celebration of the Passover, commemorating the birthnight of the nation, was customarily concluded with the singing of a group of Psalms of praise, known as the Great Hallel. Jesus and His disciples followed this custom in the night of His betrayal (Matt. 26:30).

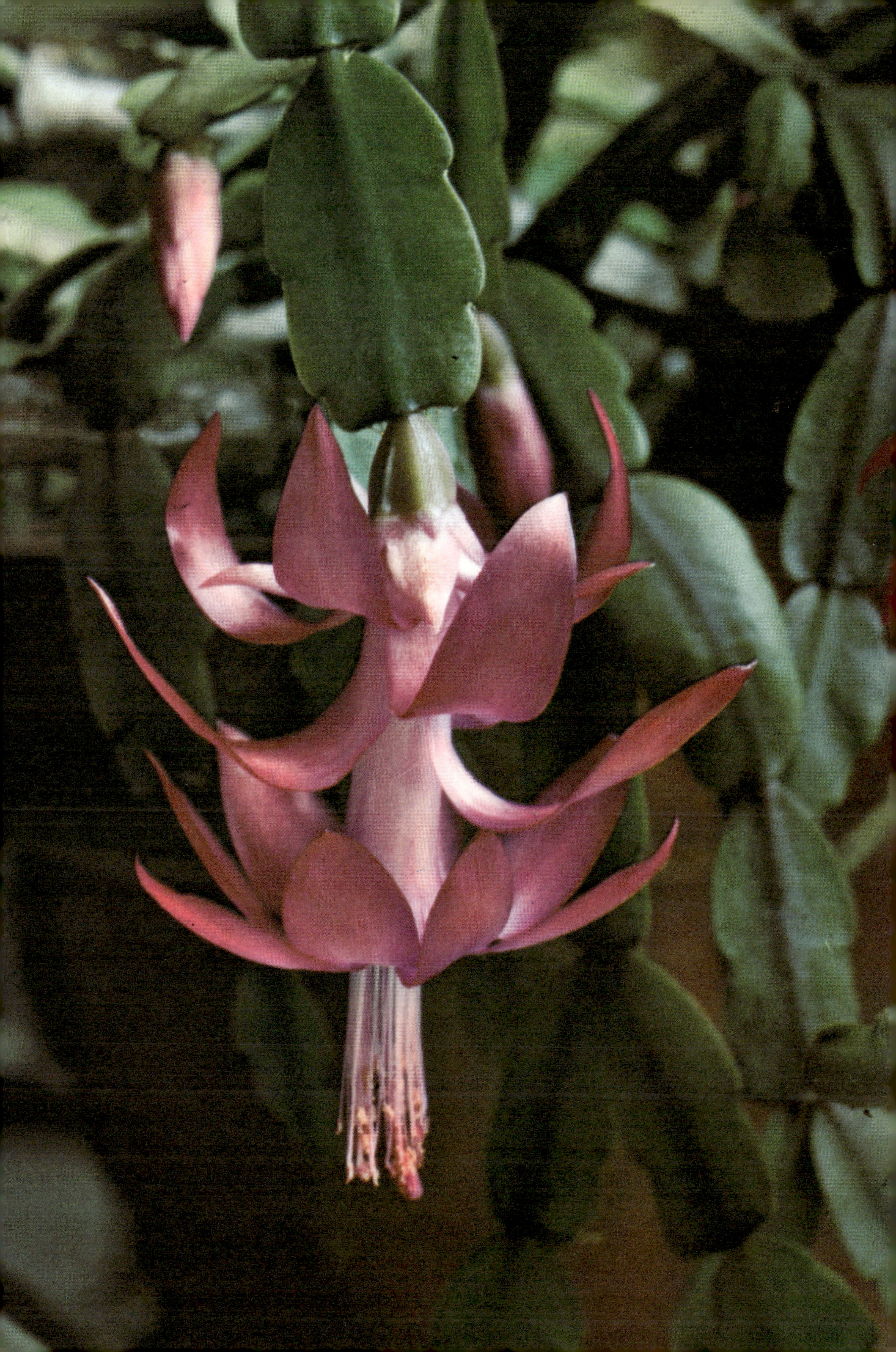

Over the years God's people have united their voices to give praise and glory unto the Lord, singing hymns and carols in their churches, schools, and homes, as well as at festive gatherings, and in recent years over the air waves. In composition these songs range from simple lyrics and impressive chorales to elaborate cantatas and musical masterpieces like Handel's "Hallelujah Chorus."

But singing to the Lord need not always be done in the company of others. We can sing to Him just as well when we are alone with none but God to hear. The housewife can praise God with song as she works by herself in the kitchen, or rocks the baby to sleep. In fact any child of God can sing to the Lord when no one else is around. God will surely be pleased with such adoration, for it is the songs that people sing in private, that really reflect their inner moods and feelings, and reveal their priorities in life.

We cannot tell whether that beautiful and charming Psalm of David, "The Lord is my Shepherd," was sung by him in his youthful years, while he was still tending his father's flock, or whether it resulted from reflection on those experiences, but we feel sure that many a moment when he was alone with his sheep was devoted to singing to the Lord.

David's songs of praise were the outpouring of a heart overflowing with gratitude for God's goodness to him. There were so many instances of that goodness in his life. He was born and reared in a family that knew and worshiped the one true God. While he was tending his flock in the wilderness he was protected from the wild lion and the bear that attacked his sheep. In his youth he was given a stunning victory over Goliath. He was repeatedly granted escape from the pursuit of king

Saul, who sought his life, and was elevated as the anointed king of God's chosen people. He enjoyed a rich measure of God's favor during his reign. Best of all, God forgave him grave sins when he penitently confessed them. Truly, God was good to him and gave him ample reason to sing unto him.

The examples of God's goodness that we can enumerate may be more modest than those of king David, but if we will carefully evaluate them we must still say that they richly deserve our songs of praise. Our heavenly Father not only provides abundantly for our needs of this earthly life, but He has also brought and kept us on the way to eternal life with Him in heaven. How can we ever adequately thank and praise Him for this marvelous grace? Our songs of praise can be the beginning that meets with His favor and prepares us for the eternal praises of heaven.

> Come ye saints, unite your praises
> With the angels round His throne;
> Soon, we hope, our God will raise us
> To the place where He is gone.
> Meet it is that we should sing,
> "Glory, glory, to our King!"
>
> Sing how Jesus came from heaven,
> How He bore the cross below,
> How all pow'r to Him is given,
> How He reigns in glory now;
> Tis a great and endless theme,
> Oh, 'tis sweet to sing of Him!

Bliss Beyond Compare

In My Father's house are many mansions: if it were not so, I would have told you. I go to prepare a place for you. And if I go and prepare a place for you, I will come again, and receive you unto Myself; that where I am, there ye may be also.

John 14:2-3

David concludes his beloved Shepherd Psalm with the upward look directed toward his heavenly home. In expectant faith he sings: "Surely goodness and mercy shall follow me all the days of my life: and I will dwell in the house of the Lord forever" (Ps. 23:6).

More than a thousand years later Jesus, the Good Shepherd, approaching the completion of His earthly mission, directed the expectation of His disciples to the same heavenly home. Preparing them for His imminent departure, He comforts them with the inviting prospect of the mansions (some call them rooms) in the Father's house above, which He Himself would make ready for them.

How these mansions will appear, what comforts they will contain, what pleasures they will provide, our imagination is not able to conceive nor our earthly understanding to comprehend. Using language familiar to us, the Bible says: "In Thy presence is fulness of joy; at Thy right hand there are pleasures for evermore" (Ps. 16:11). Certainly when Jesus prepares the mansions or rooms, they must be utterly superb and will leave nothing to be desired by "the family of God" which will be privileged to dwell there.

The inadequacy of the earthbound human mind to comprehend or human speech to convey what God has in store for His children is expressed Is. 64:4, quoted by Paul: "Eye hath not seen, nor ear heard, neither have entered into the heart of man, the things which God hath prepared for them that love Him" (1 Cor. 2:9), and again, "I knew a man in Christ above fourteen years ago, (whether in the body, I cannot tell; or whether out of the body I cannot tell: God knoweth;) . . . How that he was caught up into paradise, and heard unspeakable words, which it is not lawful for a man to utter" (2 Cor. 12:2, 4). Similarly he writes of "the glory which shall be revealed in us" (Rom. 8:18), something that far transcends our imagination. That prospect of heavenly bliss and glory keeps us from being chained to the earth.

It is, however, left to John, the beloved disciple of Jesus, to describe "the high and holy place" (Is. 57:15) where God dwells. In a most glorious symbolic vision which he received during his imprisonment on the penal isle of Patmos, with spiritual eyes he was shown the heavenly Jerusalem. "He carried me away in the spirit to a great and high mountain, and showed me that great city, the holy Jerusalem, descending out of heaven from God, having the glory of God: and her light was like unto a stone most precious, even like a jasper stone, clear as crystal; and had a wall great and high, and had twelve gates, and at the gates twelve angels, and names written thereon, which are the names of the twelve tribes of the children of Israel: on the east three gates; on the north three gates; on the south three gates; and on the west three gates. And the wall of the city had twelve foundations, and in them the names of the twelve apostles of the Lamb. And he that talked with me had a golden reed to measure the city, and the gates thereof, and the wall thereof. And the city lieth foursquare, and the length is as large as the breadth: and he measured the city with the reed, twelve thousand furlongs (1,500 miles). The length and the breadth and the height of it are equal. And he measured the wall thereof, an hundred and forty four cubits [216 feet], according to the measure of a man, that is, of the angel. And the building of the wall of it was of jasper: and the city was pure gold, like unto clear glass. And the foundations of the wall of the city were garnished with all manner of precious stones. The first foundation was jasper; the second, sapphire; the third, a chalcedony; the fourth, an emerald; the fifth, sardonyx; the sixth, sardius; the seventh, chrysolyte; the eighth, beryl; the ninth, a topaz; the tenth, a chrysoprasus; the eleventh, a jacinth; the twelfth, an amethyst. And the twelve gates were twelve pearls; every several gate was of one pearl: and the street of the city was pure gold, as it were transparent glass. And I saw no temple therein: for the Lord God Almighty and the Lamb are the temple of it. And the city had no need of the sun, neither of the moon, to shine in it: for the glory of God did lighten it, and the Lamb is the light thereof" (Rev. 21:10-23).

With awe and wonder we join Bernard of Morlas in the lines of his famous hymn.

> Jerusalem the golden,
> With milk and honey blest,
> Beneath thy contemplation
> Sink heart and voice opprest.
> I know not, oh, I know not,
> What joys await us there,
> What radiancy of glory,
> What bliss beyond compare.

Imperishable Treasure

Lay up for yourselves treasure in heaven, where neither moth nor rust consumes and where thieves do not break in and steal. For where your treasure is, there will your heart be also.
                                                              Matt. 6:20-21 RSV

Gathering and storing treasures of one kind or another is a very popular activity of the vast majority of human beings. What we consider our greatest treasure determines what kind of persons we really are.

A treasure is anything that we consider precious or valuable for its own sake, and worth making a strong effort to get and keep. That varies from person to person. What is of great value to one may not be so at all to another. For some people wealth is treasure, for others it is power and honor. For some it is a good home and family, and for others a special achievement.

The Lord does not forbid the possession of wealth or the achievement of a cherished goal. We may well acquire, use, and enjoy things of value and beauty as blessings from the hand of a loving heavenly Father, and a reflection of His goodness without counting them as our highest treasure.

Jesus bids us to set our sights higher than these things and lay up for ourselves treasures in heaven. Earthly treasures, He reminds us in the Sermon on the Mount, are perishable, and the more of them that we accumulate, the greater the temptation for thieves to break in and steal. Disasters, like fire and flood, teach us that earthly possessions can be lost very quickly. Furthermore, all are subject to change and deterioration, and finally the world and all that is in it must pass away. If our hope rests on what passes away, we have no hope left when that is gone.

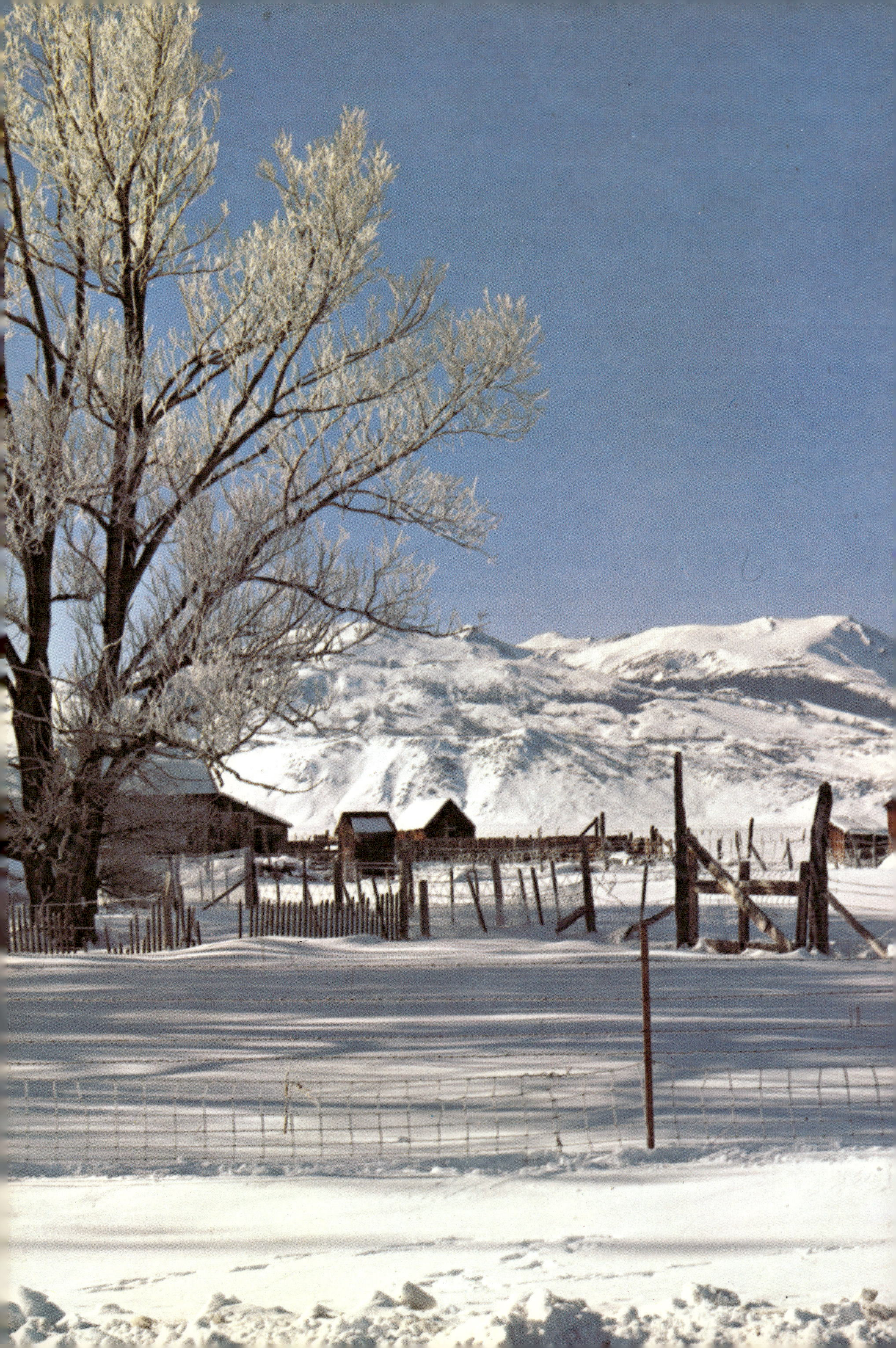

Considering this, it would seem that it should not be difficult to give priority to spiritual and heavenly things and goals. The problem is that the things of this world are so close at hand and we can see, and touch, and feel them, and they are made so very attractive and desirable by advertising and promotion. On the other hand, the things of eternity seem remote, and can only be perceived by faith. Yet just these are the imperishable treasures that our hearts should be fixed on.

What makes the right choice so critically important is the link between the treasure and the heart. Jesus points out the connection: "Where your treasure is, there will your heart be also". We just cannot set our hearts both on things of earth and things above. Our treasure and our heart are inseparable.

If God and His salvation become our foremost concern, and consequently our real treasure, our hearts will necessarily be there also. We pilgrims here on earth have a heavenly Father and a Father's house reserved in heaven for us. There also dwells our Savior who has prepared a home for us, and who has also prepared us for our home. There too dwell those whom we "love most and best."

> There at my Savior's side
> Heav'n is my home;
> I shall be glorified,
> Heav'n is my home.
> There are the good and blest,
> Those I love most and best;
> And there I, too, shall rest,
> Heav'n is my home.

The Hope of Glory

Christ in you, the hope of glory.

Col. 1:27

Hope is a prime ingredient for a happy and fulfilled life. It sustains us in times of hardship and trouble and brightens the prospect for the future. It enriches the person in possession. To be without hope is to be utterly forlorn and wretched and without any prospect for the future.

But true hope is more than a mere wish or a vanishing dream. Real hope is expectation based upon a definite promise. However, not any promise will do. Hopes based on promises of human beings are not always realized. Some bring bitter disappointment.

The Christian hope is certain because it is based on the sure promise of our faithful God. Called the "hope of glory," it is the pleasant prospect of eternal life for all believers in Christ. This is not just life eternally prolonged, but endless life in perfection and glory.

This happy prospect of unbounded hope depends entirely on our relationship with Christ. It is "Christ in you" that provides "the hope of glory." Paul refers to this relationship when writing to the Roman Christians. "If children, then heirs; heirs of God and joint-heirs with Christ; if so be that we suffer with Him, that we may be also glorified together" (Rom. 8:17). He also encouraged the Thessalonians to let their life style reflect their glorious hope. "Ye know how we exhorted and comforted and charged every one of you, as a father doth his children, that ye would walk worthy of God who hath called you into His kingdom and glory" (1 Thess. 2:11-12). He tells his beloved Philippians to look to "the Lord Jesus Christ: who shall change our vile [sin-scarred] body, that it may be fashioned like unto His glorious body" (Phil. 3:20-21). And concerning the resurrection he writes: "It is sown in dishonor, it is raised in glory" (1 Cor. 15:43).

Nor is Paul alone in expressing "the hope of glory." The apostle Peter glorifies God for our blessed Christian hope, saying; "Blessed be the God and Father of our Lord Jesus Christ, which according to His abundant mercy hath begotten us again unto a lively hope" (1 Pet. 1:3). He rejoices that he is "also a partaker of the glory that shall be revealed" (5:1), and he exhorts the elders to faithfulness and holds out the glorious hope to them that "when the chief Shepherd shall appear, ye shall receive a crown of glory that fadeth not away" (5:4). Fulfillment of this glorious hope is not due to our accomplishment, but Peter attributes it purely to "the God of all grace who hath called us unto His eternal glory by Christ Jesus" (5:10).

Jesus Himself made reference to the eternal glory of His followers when He prayed in His high-priestly prayer: "Father, I will that they also, whom Thou hast given Me, be with Me where I am; that they may behold My glory, which Thou hast given me" (Joh. 17:24).

Sharing eternal glory with our Lord and Savior is the ultimate in blessedness that we can aspire to.

> But Christ, the second Adam came
> To bear our sin and woe and shame,
> To be our Life, our Light, our Way,
> Our only Hope, our only Stay.
>
> We thank Thee, Christ; new life is ours,
> New light, new hope, new strength, new powers:
> This grace our every way attend
> Until we reach our journey's end!

Heart Transplant

A new heart also will I give you, and a new spirit will I put within you: and I will take away the stony heart out of your flesh, and I will give you a heart of flesh.

Ezek. 36:26

>Create in me a new heart, Lord,
>That gladly I obey Thy Word
>And naught, but what Thou wilt, desire;
>With such new life my soul inspire.

Heart transplants are not as new a phenomenon as many people imagine. About six centuries B.C. the prophet Ezekiel records the proposal of God to give new hearts unto people.

True, he was not referring to a medical procedure whereby surgery is employed to replace a diseased and worn out organ of the body with a healthier one removed from a victim of tragedy. However, the action that he referred to is no less remarkable and its consequences even more far reaching and lasting.

Using word pictures to help us understand an important truth, God tells us of a great and vital change that He would bring about in the lives of His people. It is described as replacing a heart of stone with one of flesh to restore them to new spiritual health and vigor.

There was an urgent need for such heart transplants. There were people in the days of Ezekiel like those in Isaiah's time of whom we read: "This people draw near Me with their mouth, and with their lips do honor Me, but have removed their heart far from Me" (Is. 29:13). They had hearts of stone, hard, cold, deceitful, and insensitive to spiritual things. For these people God had a wonderful proposal. "I will take away the stony heart out of your flesh, and I will give you a heart of flesh". He would give them a heart transplant.

God does not call for action on their part to accomplish this. They simply could not perform this operation and give themselves a new heart. Nor was there any clinic where they could go for this purpose. Only God was capable of accomplishing this. David was well aware of this when he prayed: "Create in me a clean heart, O God" (Ps. 51:10).

We all need this change of heart, for we are well aware that our hearts too are far from clean and pure, and not as tender and loving as God desires. We know how right Jesus was in His assessment of the human heart when He declared: "Out of the heart proceed evil thoughts, murders, adulteries, fornications, thefts, false witness, blasphemies" (Matt. 15:19).

It takes more than some superficial rinsing or polishing to make our hearts acceptable to God. It calls for a complete renewal or transformation. Through His almighty regenerating Word God can bring about the needed change. He can melt the hardest heart of stone and make it a heart of flesh that will reflect love for God and man.

That is the kind of heart that God wants in us. That is the kind of heart that He will implant in us if we will let Him and do not reject His divine favor. That is the kind of heart in which He consents to dwell.

> Ah, dearest Jesus, holy Child,
> Make Thee a bed, soft, undefiled,
> Within my heart, that it may be
> A quiet chamber kept for Thee.

Live Worthy of the Gospel

Only let your manner of life be worthy of the Gospel of Christ.
Phil. 1:27 RSV

The members of the Philippian church had been richly blessed through the Gospel of Christ. A mighty miracle took place in their lives when they were converted. They were freed from the slavery of sin and idolatry and made citizens of the kingdom of God and heirs of heaven.

This marvelous blessing imposed certain important obligations on them. They had the responsibility to shun their former life style with its sinful diversions and conduct, and lead a life worthy of their high calling in Christ Jesus. People should see by their behavior that they were now Christians.

The same holds true of us. We should reflect the faith we confess in the life we live. To confess that we are Christ-ians means that we should be a reflection of Christ and be careful not to bring disgrace on His holy name by what we say or do. Our whole life and conduct should live a life that is geared to the standard of God and that continues to grow and bear abundant fruit.

Sad to say, some church members are not a good recommendation for Christianity. Instead of bringing honor and respect to the messge of salvation, they bring shame and disgrace upon the Gospel of Christ by their behavior. They are often stumbling blocks for those who wish to see Jesus, when they ought to be stepping-stones on he way to the kingdom of Christ. The inconsistant lives of some church members not only give an alibi to the unbeliever but also offend many new converts.

We dare not be satisfied just to think: "I am a Christian; I know my Savior," but we are to show forth this Savior in a manner that others may also learn to know and love Him. This is not limited to a witness through words. There are many situations where actions speak louder than words. The manner of life that we live and the actions that we do should not conflict but harmonize with each other. When they show a truly Christian conduct they become a letter of recommendation of the Gospel we profess and show forth the beauty, glory, and power of the Gospel of Christ.

To achieve this goal we need constant watchfulness and fervent prayer, through which we draw upon the unlimited resource of God's divine help.

> Grant me grace, O blessed Savior,
> And Thy Holy Spirit send
> That my walk and my behavior
> May be pleasing to the end.

Unprofitable Gain

What shall it profit a man, if he shall gain the whole world, and lose his own soul? Or what shall a man give in exchange for his soul?

Mark 8:36-37

Profit and loss arouse deep interest in all walks of life. They concern not only the manufacturer and merchant but also the government and the consumer. Everyone is striving for profit or gain, and when losses exceed profits, failure results.

Profit and loss are usually thought of in terms of material things, particularly money, and it is easy to become so abosrbed in the pursuit of more and more earthly things, and heaping them up, that "the things above" are lost sight of.

This is what caused Jesus to ask the soul-searching question before us. He knew and understood human nature with its tendency to amass more and more possessions, to long for more and more luxury, to crave more and more pleasure, to aspire to more and more glory and fame, and to find deep satisfaction in acquiring them. He wants us to pause and consider the consequences of following our natural inclinations and to weigh the "world" against the "soul" when He asks: "What shall it profit a man if he shall gain the whole world, and lose his own soul? Or what shall a man give in exchange for his soul?"

The Lord has given us many wonderful things to enjoy and be grateful for in this world, but we must keep them in their proper perspective, and not make them our only goal in life or even our foremost and highest concern. That is to turn our sense of values upside down. The pursuit of earthly treasures and pleasures dare not crowd out our more important concern for our eternal salvation.

For anyone to gain "the whole world" is literally impossible. But suppose that it could be done, it would still be unprofitable gain. How long would it last? At the very most until it was removed by death, "for we brought nothing into this world, and it is certain that we can carry nothing out" (1 Tim. 6:7). When the cost of such a temporary gain is weighed against the eternal treasures sacrificed, namely heaven itself and the joys of eternity, the enormity of the gap stands out in stark reality.

Many losses can be regained or compensated for, at least in part, but there is no compensation for the loss of the soul. It cannot be recovered at any price.

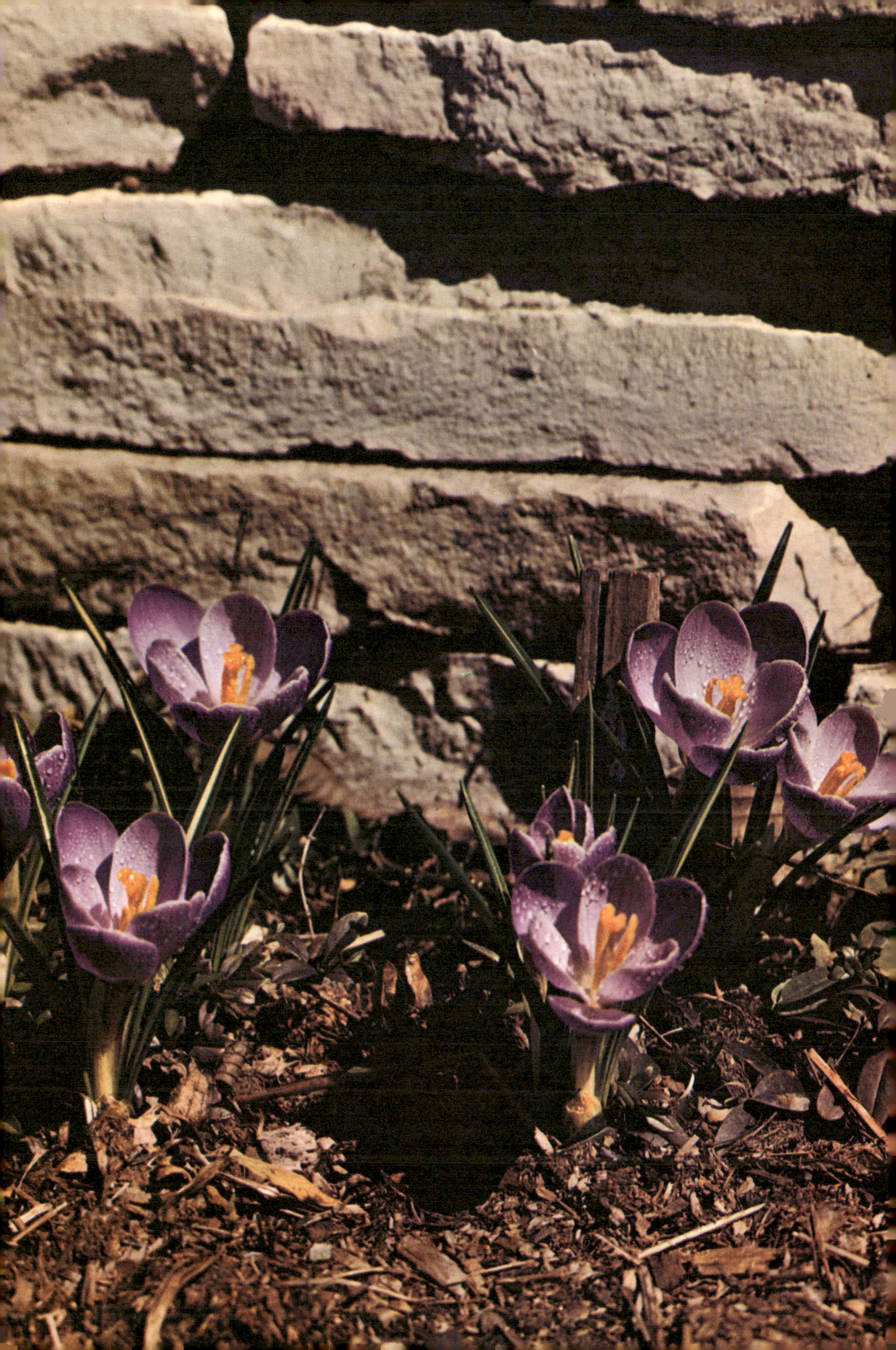

Let thoughtless thousands choose the road
That leads the soul away from God;
This happiness, dear Lord, be mine,
To live and die entirely Thine.

Fatal Neglect

How shall we escape if we neglect so great salvation?
Heb. 2:3

When the Psalmist declares that "the way of the ungodly shall perish" (1:6), he states a plain and simple fact that everyone can understand. The same is true when the prophet Ezekiel proclaims the Word of the Lord: "Repent, and turn yourselves from all your transgressions; so iniquity shall not be your ruin" (Ezek. 18:30). Wickedness and vice are generally recognized as causes of damnation. What is often overlooked and forgotten, however, is that many more people will be lost because of indifference, carelessness, or negligence, than because of wickedness.

God has gone to great lengths to prepare a great salvation for us. He spared not His own Son but freely delivered Him up for us all. He made it easy for us to partake of this salvation. Whoever believes in Jesus Christ as his or her personal Savior shall not perish but have eternal life.

Some, of course, refuse God's way of salvation in favor of their own merit or righteousness by which they want to lay claim to eternal life. Some reject Christ Jesus outright and will have nothing to do with Him or are openly hostile toward Him. Others deny the one true God and follow after idols. All this is tragic indeed, but no more tragic than the sad story of the great multitude of people who do not avail themselves of this great salvation simply because they do not care enough about it. They are so much concerned about material things, making money, the management of their business, the comfort of their home, their standard of living, and the pursuit of amusements, that the things that relate to their salvation are either pushed into the background or completely forgotten.

This is not a special sign of our modern age in which we live. It dates back to earliest times. Jesus found that same spirit of indifference toward spiritual things prevalent during His earthly life, and He taught the people to put first things first by being more concerned about the kingdom of God than about food, drink, and clothing. In His parables He showed the folly of forgetting about the soul while planning larger barns to store the bountiful crops that the Lord had given, and of being so much devoted to the concern for fields, oxen, and family, that the invitation to the great feast at the heavenly banquet table was spurned.

However, the wide prevalence of the neglect of salvation does not excuse anyone., How can we hope to escape the consequence of indifference to the one supreme thing which every sinner needs when the opportunities to respond abound so richly.

> Sinners, turn; why will you die?
> God, your Maker, asks you—Why?
> God, who did your being give,
> Made you with Himself to live.
>
> He the fatal cause demands,
> Asks the work of His own hands,
> Why, you thankless creatures, why
> Will you cross His love and die?
>
> Will you not His grace receive?
> Will you still refuse to live?
> O you long-sought sinners, why
> Will you grieve your God and die?

The Cloak of Humility

Be clothed with humility: for God resisteth the proud and giveth grace to the humble.

1 Peter 5:5

From time to time lists of the "best dressed" men and women in the country are published, and it is considered quite an honor to make it. A far higher distinction than this is to make God's "best dressed" list. However, that does not call for the latest fashions of the world's top designers, but rather that we wear the cloak of humility.

But many judge quite differently. To them humility seems drab and dingy, cheap and unattractive. They consider it demeaning, appropriate only for the weak and servile, and they would not be seen in it. They would rather bask in the robe of pride, parade in it with a feeling of importance and superiority before an admiring public, and look with disdain upon the less fortunate. In contrast to this haughty attitude Scripture teaches that "God resisteth the proud and giveth grace to the humble."

The prophet Micah asks the appropriate and vital question: "With what shall I come before the Lord?" (6:6 RSV). In response he rules out the ordinary offerings favored in his day, such as yearling calves, rams, and olive oil. He rejects the idea of satisfying God with the sacrifice of the firstborn. Then he reminds that God has already given the answer: "He has showed you, O man, what is good; and what does the Lord require of you but to do justice, and to love kindness, and to walk humbly with your God?" (6:8 RSV).

All that God asks His people to do is to *walk with* Him, and in harmony with His will and pleasure, doing justice for the oppressed, showing warmhearted, compassionate love, and not least, exercising genuine humility.

Our finest example in humility is furnished by our Lord and Savior Himself, who put aside His divine prerogatives when He took our human nature, humbled Himself, and lived a life of utter obedience. Jesus showed real humility throughout His earthly life. He worked in a carpenter shop until He was ready to assume His public ministry. Going about in the form and likeness of a servant, He could say of Himself: "The foxes have holes, and the birds of the air have nests; but the Son of Man hath not where to lay His head" (Matt. 8:20). When strife erupted among His disciples because the mother of James and John sought preference over the others for her two sons, Jesus directed them to His own example of humility: "Whosoever will be chief among you, let him be your servant; even as the Son of Man came not to be ministered unto, but to minister, and to give His life a ransom for many" (Matt. 20:26-28). While He possessed all majesty and power by divine right, He voluntarily laid them aside to complete the redemption of sinful mankind. Instead of a display of royal pomp and glory, His Palm Sunday entrance into Jerusalem was made on a lowly beast of burden. When his disciples scrambled for places of honor at the Passover table, the Master gave them an example in humility by performing the duty of the lowliest servant and washing their feet.

The subject of humility was one that came up often in His teachings because of the constant need for it. Thus in the parable of the Pharisee and the publican He declared: "Everyone that exalteth himself shall be abased; and he that humbleth himself shall be exalted"

(Luke 18:14). The apostles followed the Master's footsteps by exhorting their followers to humility.

Times have not changed in this respect. God still "giveth grace to the humble."

> Fairest and best adorned is she
> Whose clothing is humility.

Humility best shows itself in willing and humble service. It is not determined by the type of service rendered, but by the spirit in which it is done.

> The humble heart and lowly
> God lifteth up on high;
> Beneath His feet in anguish
> The haughty soul shall lie.
> The heart sincere and right,
> That heeds God's invitation
> And makes true preparation,
> It is the Lord's delight.

What Is Truth?

Pilate saith unto Him, What is truth?

John 18:38

This scornful question of Pontius Pilate at the trial of Jesus has been echoed by countless cyncial people. Implying that there is no absolute truth, Pilate did not wait for an answer, but hurried back outside to the Jews. He had no time to discuss so speculative a subject.

Many, like the Roman governor, doubt the existence of final truth and consider the search for it bewildering and futile. They have been confused by contradictory claims for what has been called truth. Others have graspingly searched for final truth and have ended in blind alleys because they have followed the wrong leads.

The consensus of public opinion does not supply the answer since it is not trustworthy. Human reason is no better because it too is fallible. Scientific research can indeed reveal exact and authentic data in the realm of nature and history, but final truth lies beyond its scope.

What then is truth? And can it be found?

There is absolute truth and it is possible for us to find it if we look for it in the right place. Jesus, the only begotten Son of God, provided the answer on the evening before Pilate asked the question. In His highpriestly prayer, addressed to the heavenly Father He declared: "Thy Word is truth" (John 17:17).

God's Word, as we have it in the Bible, is truth. From it we learn the eternal and unchanging truths concerning God and man, as God Himself has revealed them. It contains the fundamental truths that are critical for us—the truth concerning ourselves and our sin, the truth concerning God and His love, the truth concerning earth and heaven, and the truth concerning time and eternity. These truths not only can be known, but they are known because they are revealed in His Word.

But Jesus has even more to tell us about truth. Before Pilate asked his memorable question, Jesus, in His farewell conversation with His disciples, declared: "I am the Way, the Truth, and the Life" (John 14:6). He did not say, I will show you where you can find the truth. He said "I am the Truth." He was the eternal Word by which God made Himself known in His power, in His love, and in His glory. Twice the heavenly Father had put the seal of divine approval on Him by calling Him His beloved Son in whom He was well pleased (Matt. 3:17; 17:5). "Hear ye Him!" His Word is Truth.

It was most fitting that Jesus should tell Pilate: "To this end was I born, and for this cause came I into the world, that I should bear witness unto the truth. Everyone that is of the truth heareth My voice" (John 18:37).

He, the Truth, has shown His disciples and us how to acquire and possess the eternal truth. "If ye continue in My Word, then are ye My disciples indeed; and ye shall know the truth, and the truth shall make you free" (John 8:31-32).

No one who hears His Word and believes in Him will ever be in darkness, neither here nor hereafter.

> Thou art the Truth; Thy Word alone
> True wisdom can impart;
> Thou only canst inform the mind
> And purify the heart.
>
> Thou art the Way, the Truth, the Life;
> Grant us the Way to know,
> That Truth to keep, that Life to win,
> Whose joys eternal flow.

But Not

We are troubled on every side, yet not distressed; we are perplexed, but not in despair; persecuted, but not forsaken; cast down, but not destroyed.

4 Cor. 4:8-9

Trouble and heartache are not new in the history of mankind, nor are God's children exempt from them. Job, a loyal follower of God who endured an overflowing measure of grief, said: "Man that is born of a woman is of few days and full of trouble" (14:1). Moses, who was chosen by God to lead His people out of slavery in Egypt, wrote: "The days of our years are threescore years and ten; and if by reason of strength they be fourscore years, yet is their strength labor and sorrow; for it is soon cut off, and we fly away" (Ps. 90:10). Asaph, choirmaster under David, lamented that he had to endure torment and punishment while the ungodly seemed to prosper and live in comfort (Ps. 73). And the apostle Paul had many troubles and hardships in his career. All of these experienced what Paul expressed so well; they were troubled, *yet not* distressed (hemmed in); perplexed, *but not* in despair; persecuted, *but not* forsaken; cut down, *but not* destroyed, or as we read in one of the newer translations, knocked down, *but not* out.

Their good fortune was not due either to their own superior wisdom or outstanding skill or power nor to the might of strong friends or allies. They had a far greater resource to rely on for support and deliverance. They shared the spirit of David in praise of past deliverance, and exhuberant confidence for the future. "The Lord is my light and my salvation; whom shall I fear? The Lord is the strength of my life; of whom shall I be afraid? ... though host should encamp against me, my heart shall not fear ... Wait on the Lord: be of good courage, and He shall strengthen thine heart; wait, I say, on the Lord" (Ps. 27:1, 3, 14).

Many things have changed in the course of time since these servants of God experienced the Lord's supporting presence in their need, but God's loving concern for His chldren and His faithfulness in keeping His promises of safety and protection of His own are not among them. They are unchangeable. Whatever condition we as His children may find ourselves in, we can comfort ourselves with the absolute assurance that the eternal Father in heaven never abandons His own. Our situation may sometimes be bad, even very bad, *but not* so bad that we must despair. Our faith is firmly grounded in the knowledge of Christ's suffering and death for us and the certainty of His triumphant resurrection, which gives us the firm hope and assurance of our own resurrection and the blessed prospect of eternal life and glory in heaven.

> If thou but suffer God to guide thee
> And hope in Him through all thy ways,
> He'll give thee strength, whate'er betide thee,
> And bear thee through the evil days.
> Who trusts in God's unchanging love
> Builds on a rock that naught can move.
>
> Sing, pray, and keep His ways unswerving,
> Perform thy duties faithfully,
> And trust His Word; though undeserving,
> Thou shalt yet find it true for thee.
> God never yet forsook in need
> The soul that trusted Him indeed.

What Time Is It?

The end of all things is at hand; be ye therefore sober, and watch unto prayer.

1 Peter 4:7

What time is it? That is one of the most common questions asked and heard. There are innumerable reasons for asking the question. People are anxious to know whether they will be in time for an appointment. They want to know how long before they go on or off the job. They wonder whether it is not time to eat again.

Everybody seems to have this question on the mind and lips. Yet many people seem quite unconcerned about the really important aspect of the question. They are so busy with those little segments of time that we call seconds, minutes, and hours, that they lose sight of the end of time, which is irresistibly drawing nearer and nearer.

What time is it? St. Peter answers: "The end of all things is at hand." We are living in the last days. The signs of the time clearly point to that. Ere long must come the time when "day and night come to an end" (Job 26:10), "that there should be time no longer" (Rev. 10:6).

It is a time for watchfulness. Because "the time is short" (1 Cor. 7:29), we should give close attention to the exhortation of St. Peter: "Be ye therefore sober, and watch unto prayer." We should be careful to maintain a steady, well-balanced conduct and keep our mind clear and sound. We should be ever watchful so that we are not caught off guard when our time runs out. "This know also, that in the last days perilous times shall come" (2 Tim. 3:1).

It is a time for prayer. By exhorting to prayer the apostle is reminding us of our relation to God and our complete dependence on Him. The words of warning spoken by Jesus to His disciples in Gethsemane also apply in these last days: "Watch and pray, that ye enter not into temptation" (Matt. 26:41).

It is a time for grace. The Lord is still calling to repentance. He is still offering His grace and forgiveness. It is not yet too late. The Lord may still be found. "Behold, now is the accepted time; behold, now is the day of salvation" (2 Cor. 6:2). It is the utmost folly to cast away or squander the time of grace in the expectation that we shall have plenty of opportunity to turn to the Lord at some future time. We "know neither the day nor the hour wherein the Son of Man cometh" (Matt. 25:13). Then there will be no time for preparation.

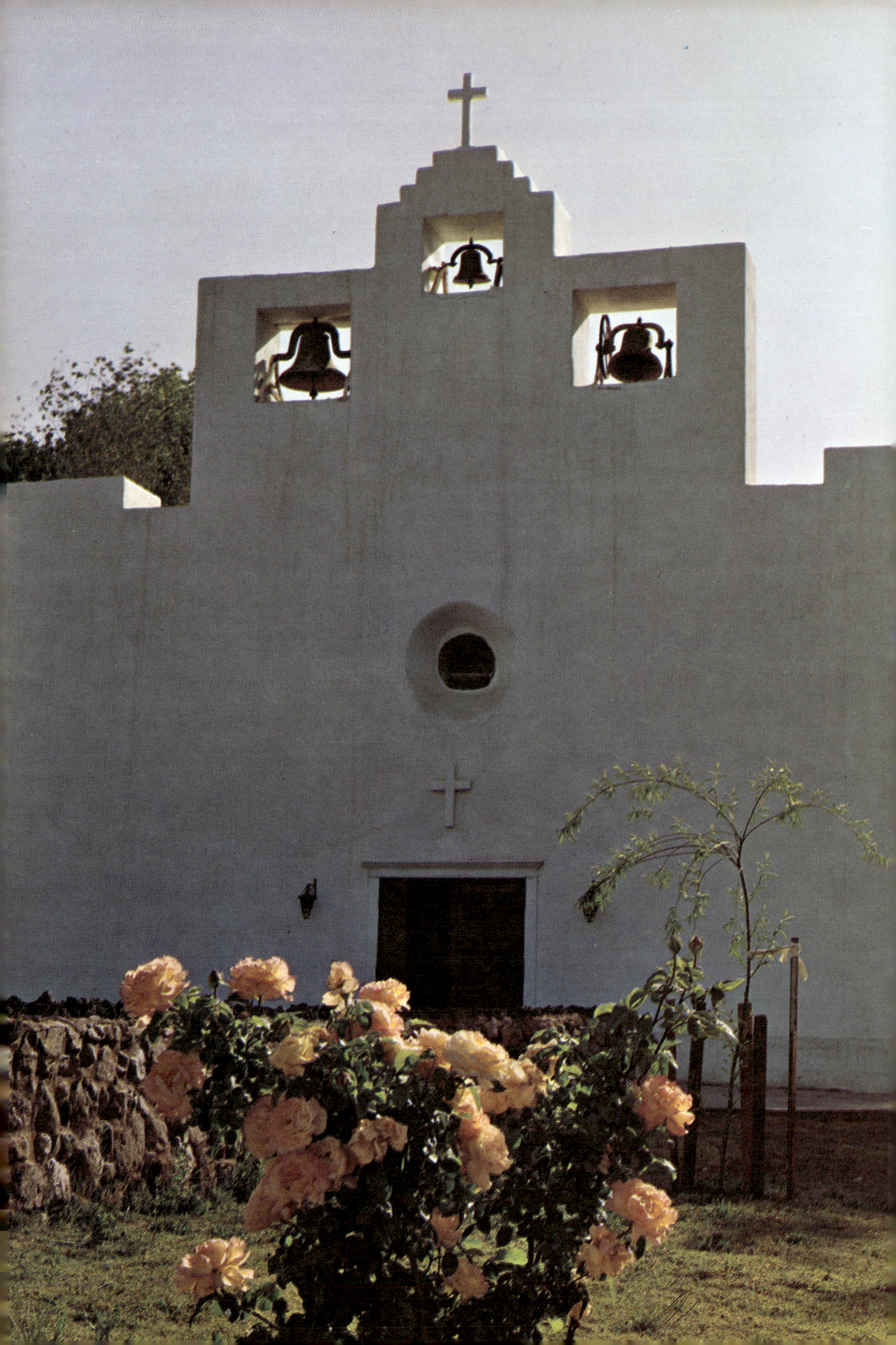

An instantaneous change will take place "in a moment, in the twinkling of an eye" (1 Cor. 15:52).

It is a time for doing. The Lord expects more from His followers than that they should occupy space in His church or adorn it. He has work for us to do. "We are His workmanship, created in Christ Jesus unto good works, which God hath before ordained that we should walk in them" (Eph. 2:10). Such talent and strength as the Lord has given and preserved to us are to be placed into His service to lead and direct others to Christ Jesus, their Savior. The shortness of the time must spur us on, as the apostle states: "Redeeming the time, because the days are evil" (Eph. 5:16). Ever urging us on to make the best use of our allotted time is the example of Jesus, who said: "I must work the works of Him that sent Me, while it is day; the night cometh, when no man can work" (John 9:4).

What time is it? It is later than you think. The line which divides time and eternity is near the point of being dissolved.

> Who knows when death may overtake me!
> Time passes on, my end draws near.
> How swiftly can my breath forsake me!
> How soon can life's last hour appear!
> My God, for Jesus' sake I pray
> Thy peace may bless my dying day.

Amen

All the people shall say, Amen.

Deut. 27:26

The word Amen is said to be part of more languages than any other word spoken in this wide world of ours. The first recorded use of the word was about 3,500 years ago, near the end of the long wilderness journey of the children of Israel, as they were about to enter and occupy the Promised Land. In a series of addresses given by Moses he recalled the great events of the Exodus and the years spent in the wilderness. He refreshed their memory of God's covenant with His people and reviewed the laws by which they were to be governed. The people responded by ratifying the covenant and pledging obedience to the laws. In at least some instances the response included the word, Amen. It meant certainly, truly, surely. By it they gave their wholehearted approval to the message of Moses.

In the course of time it became common usage to respond to the praise of God and prayers with Amen. Thus in the synogogues and the early church it was customary to say AMEN to the prayers of the rabbis or pastors.

It is evident that Amen was a favorite word of Jesus. The New Testament records no less than 103 times (25 times by John alone) that He used the word. It was also used frequently by the apostles and its usage has come down to us through the centuries.

When used at the beginning of a sentence Amen means verily or truly, and when it is repeated it gains the force of a superlative with the meaning, most assuredly. At the end of a prayer it expresses the firm persuasion or trust in God's ability and readiness to hear our prayers. So Luther says in his Small Catechism: "I should be certain that these petitions are acceptable to our Father in heaven, and are heard by Him; for He Himself has commanded us so to pray, and has promised to hear us. Amen, Amen, that is yea, yea, it shall be so." Amen is in effect a separate prayer, giving emphasis and approval to the foregoing petition.

Beside the customary usage of the word, the Bible also uses Amen as a name for God Himself. Thus Isaiah writes: "He who invokes a blessing on himself in the land shall do so by the God whose name is Amen, and he who utters an oath in the land shall do so by the God of Amen" (Is. 65:16 NEB). (Some versions have translated the Hebrew "God of Amen" as "the God of Truth.") In the New Testament Amen is used as a name of Christ. "These things saith the Amen, the faithful and true Witness, the Beginning of the creation of God" (Rev. 3:14). And St. Paul writes to the Corinthian Christians: "All the promises of God in Him are yea, and in Him Amen, unto the glory of God" (2 Cor. 1:20). Because Christ is the fulfillment of all the divine promises, therefore He is also the Amen, and the Truth.

> Praise to the Lord! Oh, let all that
>   is in me adore Him!
> All that hath life and breath, come now
>   with praises before Him!
> Let the Amen
> Sound from His people again;
> Gladly for aye we adore Him.

Millions of people live and act as though there is no God, and never utter a word of prayer, and consequently never use the word. For some who do pray, even regularly, Amen means nothing more than an emphatic period at the close of their prayer to signal that it is ended. But where the meaning of Amen is rightly understood it becomes the stamp of our sincerity and an expression of our confidence that God, who has commanded us to pray and has promised to hear us, will certainly answer our prayers in His own way and at His own time for our temporal and eternal good.

> Amen, that is, So shall it be.
> Confirm our faith and hope in Thee
> That we may doubt not, but believe
> What here we ask we shall receive.
> Thus in Thy name and at Thy word
> We say: Amen. Oh, hear us, Lord!